2-14-75

Shakespeare Vignettes:

ADAPTATIONS FOR ACTING

Shakespeare Vignettes:

ADAPTATIONS FOR ACTING

by Albert Johnson

VIGNETTE VERSIONS OF WILLIAM SHAKE-
SPEARE'S BEST-KNOWN PLAYS, EDITED AND
ARRANGED FOR CLASSROOM STUDY AND FOR
STAGE AND TELEVISION PERFORMANCE. A
LIVELY AND SUCCINCT TREATMENT OF:

The Merchant of Venice
The Taming of the Shrew
Romeo and Juliet
Macbeth
Hamlet
Othello

SOUTH BRUNSWICK AND NEW YORK:
A. S. Barnes and Company
LONDON: Thomas Yoseloff Ltd

Library of Congress Catalogue Card Number: 79-88273

A. S. Barnes and Co., Inc.
Cranbury, New Jersey 08512

Thomas Yoseloff Ltd
108 New Bond Street
London W1Y OQX, England

SBN 498 06768 8
Printed in the United States of America

TO THE MEMORY OF MADRE

Contents

Introduction

This carefully considered condensation of six of the best-known and best-loved plays by William Shakespeare is designed to fill a cultural need that is not ordinarily met in the quickening pace of our diversified society. With the increasing emphasis on science, which our technological civilization demands, there seems less and less opportunity for exposure to that area of our heritage which has historically given depth to individual character and breadth to the art of living.

While it is true that no abridgment of any work of literature is a satisfactory substitute for the full text, it is equally true that some exposure to a work is better than none, and it is hoped and expected that familiarity with these vignette versions of the Bard's plays will stimulate interest in depth study of the plays and, even where further study is not forthcoming, that the vignette versions will give background for thought and conversation in an area of learning which educated people presumably have in common.

Because each play in vignette form can be read or reenacted within a thirty-minute period, a whole series of plays can be studied in a semester course and students should gain a much wider understanding of the scope of Shakespeare than is possible through the study of one or two plays during the course of a semester.

Meticulous and creative effort has gone into the preparation of the vignette versions, with the intent to faithfully adhere to the main story and preserve the mood and literary style. The object has been to hew to a clear, straight story line, eliminating subplots, and to retain wherever feasible the literary gems often referred to as "purple patches."

Each vignette, having been through the rigors of both stage and television production, is readily and easily playable by either experienced or inexperienced players. The plays may be performed in the classroom or for the public on an amateur basis without special permission, but are not available for commercial or professional use without the securing of performance rights. Each play is prefaced by a brief synopsis of the action.

That legion of teachers who find themselves having to teach Shakespeare with inadequate background may find the teaching aids in the appendix of the collection to be useful in leading class discussion of the various plays. The appendix also includes biographical data on William Shakespeare and some special comments on the Elizabethan period in juxtaposition to the world civilization of Shakespeare's time.

When all the vignette versions have been read, studied, or performed, there is this to reread, reconsider, and remember—this quotation from the first folio of Shakespeare's plays edited and published by his fellow players in 1616:

> It is not our province who only gather his works and give them you to praise him. It is yours who read him, and there we hope to your diverse capacities you will find enough both to draw and hold you, for his wit could no more lie hid than it could be lost. Read him, therefore, and again and again, and if then you do not like him surely you are in some manifest danger not to understand him.

Shakespeare Vignettes:
ADAPTATIONS FOR ACTING

1

THE MERCHANT OF VENICE

The Merchant of Venice

Synopsis

In the Venice of long ago lived the merchant Antonio, who borrowed money from the venerable Shylock to help his young friend, Bassanio, woo and wed a renowned and wealthy beauty named Portia. Of all her many suitors, Bassanio is Portia's favorite, but will he come again to woo her?

Assuredly he will, if he can raise the funds for such a venture. Antonio, whose ships are all at sea, is out of cash, but his credit is good, and there is Shylock, who lives by lending money.

Three thousand ducats is the sum required, for three months. Antonio is a good man, Shylock admits, but he cannot resist taunting Bassanio and Antonio because they, Christians, come to borrow money of him whom they have called a cut-throat dog. Knowing that they are at his mercy, and possessing a perverse sense of humor, Shylock finally agrees to lend the money, providing Antonio will put up as bond a pound of his fair flesh, to be cut from his body where it most pleases the curmudgenly Shylock. Bassanio considers such a deal ridiculous, but Antonio assures him that his ships will all be back within two months and he can pay off the loan in ample time, so off Shylock goes to get the ducats.

Soon Bassanio is off to Belmont where Portia lives, and with him is his friend Gratiano, who insists on tagging along for reasons of his own. Another friend, Lorenzo, has fallen for none other than Jessica, the pretty daughter of old Shylock. Abetted by young Launcelot, the rascally servant of Shylock, the two exchange love messages, resulting, inevitably, in an elopement, and Jessica's absconding with all the family gold and jewels.

Having loaned the Christians money, Shylock now finds that his own daughter has been abducted by a Christian. He is angry, bitter, and heartbroken. He sends his old friend, Tubal, to look for the runaway couple. His search is fruitless, but he brings the news that Antonio's ships have met with disaster on the seas and the famous merchant of Venice is ruined. "I am very glad of it," says Shylock. "I'll plague him; I'll torture him: I am glad of it."

Jeered in the streets, Shylock is asked what he will do with a pound of Antonio's flesh. "If it will feed nothing else," he says, "it will feed my revenge." He vows to execute the villainy taught him by the Christians as he eagerly awaits the trial.

While Shylock thunders and storm clouds hang ominously over Antonio in Venice, Belmont is sun-filled with the joy of a betrothal. The gracious, brilliant Portia has given herself and all her wealth to the handsome Bassanio, and Gratiano has won the hand of Portia's maid and companion, Nerissa. The sun, however, is suddenly eclipsed when the news reaches Bassanio of Antonio's bankruptcy and Shylock's foreclosure. With his friend's life thus in danger, Bassanio must go at once to be present at the trial, and, explaining the whole affair to Portia, he begs her leave to go. Sharing his sorrows with his joys, she graciously grants leave and says that she and Nerissa will await the return of Bassanio and Gratiano, both of whom wear the betrothal that they are pledged never to lose or give away.

Inventive as she is adorable and wise, Portia contrives a way to be helpful at Antonio's trial. To the amazement and delight of Nerissa, she announces to her that they two will borrow robes from her Justice uncle and go as judge and clerk.

Introduced at the Venice trial as a young and learned doctor of law, Portia proceeds to try the case, while Nerissa serves as court clerk, both being so disguised that they are not recognizable by any present. However, as the "learned doctor" studies the case, Portia realizes that she has a knottier problem than she expected. The law is clear. Shylock's demand is just. Clearly Antonio must sacrifice a pound of his flesh, and with it, obviously, his life. In an effort to appeal to Shylock's humanity, Portia pleads with him to be merciful, and to remember that the quality of mercy is not a thing that can be strained, but Shylock, who is thoroughly impressed with the young judge's knowledge of the law and insistence upon justice, declares he will have his payment of the bond, his pound of flesh.

A pound of Antonio's flesh to be cut off nearest the heart! The law allows it and the court awards it! The words come hard for Portia but the case is clear. Shylock, jubilant, his knife ready, rushes toward the bared and waiting breast of Antonio. Suddenly he is intercepted by Judge Portia.

"Tarry a little," she says. "This bond doth give thee here no jot of blood." He can cut his pound of flesh, but if he spills one ounce of blood in the process, his lands and goods will be confiscated by the State. So reads the law!

At this, the courtroom, filled with Antonio's friends, is jubilant. "Give me my principle and let me go," cries Shylock, but since he refused payment offered him earlier, the learned judge rules that he can have nothing, and points out that he is in danger of his life, since he has violated a state law that says that anyone who contrives against the life of a citizen stands at the mercy of the Duke only. The Duke is quick to pardon Shylock his life, to show the difference between his standards and those of Shylock. Broken in will, though not in spirit, Shylock begs leave to quit the court on the grounds that he is not well. Send the document after him, he says, and he will sign it.

Antonio and Bassanio rush to the youthful judge to tender their thanks and offer some payment, but Portia and Nerissa, eager to depart before their identity is discovered, refuse payment. As a ruse, Portia requests instead the ring she has earlier given Bassanio! Later we discover that the clerk, Nerissa, has also managed to get her ring from Gratiano. This makes for high comedy later.

In Belmont Lorenzo and Jessica, who have found their way to the hospitality of Portia's mansion, are enjoying the idyllic night when Portia and Nerissa return, soon to be followed by Bassanio, Gratiano, and Antonio, whom Bassanio wants his bride to meet. Soon it is discovered that the men are without their rings, and the ladies taunt them unmercifully when they squirm and try to explain that they gave the rings to the judge and clerk at their insistence.

At last Portia explains that she was the learned judge and Nerissa the clerk. They produce the rings in proof and all ends in merriment.

The Merchant of Venice

(Video directions are in italics)

Note: The Narrator may play several of the incidental roles, in which case the following should be inserted in the Narrator's first speech: "I am the Narrator in this short version of the play, but in the telling of the tale I am actor, too, so you will see me first as one character, then another."

Longshot including Antonio, Bassanio, Gratiano, and Lorenzo. During the following Narration the men stroll very slowly from upstage toward the camera as they engage in pantomime of animated conversation as they approach the camera. Antonio is obviously the center of attraction and in a moment Gratiano and Lorenzo take their leave as Antonio and Bassanio wave them off. Then Antonio and Bassanio stroll to a nearby bench, where they seat themselves and continue their pantomimic conversation.

NARRATOR: *(off camera)*

The Merchant of Venice by William Shakespeare has been called the Bard's most controversial comedy. Some have called it anti-Jewish, others have called it anti-Christian. It seems unlikely that Shakespeare meant it to be anti-anybody. Even in this brief vignette version we sense his great compassion for human beings with all their faults and virtues. There are the gay young Lords of Venice who hang about Antonio, the wealthy merchant. They are young men of virtue, but also opportunists. Young Lord Bassanio, for instance, touches Antonio for a loan so he can woo the brilliant, affluent Portia, to whom he has quite lost his heart. Antonio is out of ready cash, but he will go Bassanio's bond if money can be found.

Antonio and Bassanio rise. Antonio puts a hand on Bassanio's shoulder.

NARRATOR:

"Try what my credit can in Venice do," he says, and Bassanio's fancies fly hopefully again toward Belmont, where Portia and her maid, Nerissa, talk merrily of suitors.

Dissolve to two-shot of Portia and Nerissa

NERISSA:

Do you not remember, lady, in your father's time, a Venetian, a scholar, and a soldier?

PORTIA:

Yes, yes, it was Bassanio; as I think he was so called.

NERISSA:

True, Madam: he, of all the men that ever my foolish eyes looked upon, was the best deserving a fair lady.

PORTIA:

I remember him well; and I remember him worthy of thy praise.

Close-up of Portia dissolving to close-up of Shylock during the following

NARRATOR:

But before he can go to Belmont to woo fair Portia, Bassanio must find money. Well, there is old Shylock, the moneylender. Shylock, the rich, parsimonious Jew.

Medium shot of Bassanio and Shylock standing some distance from each other

SHYLOCK:

Three thousand ducats for three months, and Antonio bound.

BASSANIO:

Your answer to that.

SHYLOCK:

Antonio is a good man.

BASSANIO:

Have you heard any imputation to the contrary?

SHYLOCK:

Ho, no, no, no, no: my meaning in saying he is a good man, is to have you understand me, that he is sufficient. Yet his means are in supposition: he hath an argosy bound to Tripolis, another to the Indies; I understand, morever, upon the Rialto, that he hath a third at Mexico, a fourth for England, and other ventures he hath, squandered abroad. The man is, notwithstanding, sufficient. What news on the Rialto? Who is he comes here?

Antonio enters

BASSANIO:

This is Signior Antonio.

ANTONIO:

Well, Shylock, shall we be beholding to you?

Camera close on Shylock

SHYLOCK:

Signior Antonio, many a time and oft
In the Rialto you have rated me
About my moneys and my usances:
Still have I borne it with a patient shrug;
For sufferance is the badge of all our tribe.
You call me misbeliever, cut-throat dog,
And spit upon my Jewish gaberdine,
And all for use of that which is mine own.
Well then, it now appears you need my help:
Go to, then; you come to me, and you say
"Shylock, we would have moneys:" you say so;
You, that did void your rheum upon my beard,
And foot me as you spurn a stranger cur
Over your threshold: moneys is your suit.
What should I say to you? Should I not say
"Hath a dog money? is it possible
A cur can lend three thousand ducats?" or
Shall I bend low and in a bondman's key,
With bated breath and whispering humbleness,
Say this—
"Fair sir, you spit on me on Wednesday last;
You spurn'd me such a day; another time
You called me a dog; and for these courtesies
I'll lend you thus much moneys?"
Medium shot of Shylock, Antonio, and Bassanio

ANTONIO:

I am as like to call thee so again,
To spit on thee again, to spurn thee too.
If thou wilt lend this money, lend it not
As to thy friends; for when did friendship take
A breed for barren metal of his friend?
But lend it rather to thine enemy;

Who if he break, thou mayst with better face
Exact the penalty.

SHYLOCK:

Why, look you, how you storm!
I would be friends with you, and have you love,
Forget the shames that you have stain'd me with,
Supply your present wants, and take no doit
Of usance for my moneys, and you'll not hear me:
This is kind I offer.

BASSANIO:

This were kindness.

Close on Shylock

SHYLOCK:

This kindness will I show.
Go with me to a notary, seal me there
Your single bond; and, in a merry sport,
If you repay me not on such a day,
In such a place, such sum or sums as are
Express'd in the condition, let the forfeit
Be nominated for an equal pound
Of your fair flesh . . .

*Camera close on Bassanio for his reaction, then shift to
Antonio for his line and reaction*

. . . to be cut off and taken
In what part of your body pleaseth me.

ANTONIO:

Content, i'faith: I'll seal to such a bond,
And say there is much kindness in the Jew.

*Dolly back for medium shot of Antonio, Bassanio, and
Shylock*

BASSANIO:

You shall not seal to such a bond for me;
I'll rather dwell in my necessity.

ANTONIO:

Why, fear not, man; I will not forfeit it:
Within these two months, that's a month before
This bond expires, I do expect return
Of thrice three times the value of this bond.

SHYLOCK:

Then meet me forthwith at the notary's;
Give him direction for this merry bond;
And I will go and purse the ducats straight.

Shylock exits, Antonio and Bassanio start off but Bassanio is detained by Gratiano, who has entered in time to hear the last part of the above dialogue.

GRATIANO:

Signior Bassanio!

BASSANIO:

Gratiano!

GRATIANO:

I must go with you to Belmont.

BASSANIO:

Why, then you must.

Bassanio and Antonio exeunt and camera holds on Gratiano for an expression of happy expectation. Dissolve to medium shot of Jessica and Launcelot. Jessica gestures to Launcelot who comes close to her.

NARRATOR: *(during the above shot)*

The deal is on. But something else is going on that Shylock knows not of. Something concerning his pretty and rebellious daughter, Jessica.

Two-shot of Jessica and Launcelot

JESSICA:

Launcelot, soon at supper shalt thou see Lorenzo.
Give him this letter; do it secretly.

LAUNCELOT:

If a Christian do not play the knave, and get thee,

I am much deceived.

JESSICA:

Farewell, good Launcelot.

Launcelot exits and camera comes close on Jessica.

JESSICA:

O Lorenzo, If thou keep promise, I shall end
this strife, become a Christian, and thy loving
wife.

*Dissolve to two-shot of Launcelot and Lorenzo. Lorenzo
has just finished reading Jessica's note.*

LORENZO:

Tell gentle Jessica I will not fail her.

*Dissolve to long shot of Shylock pacing and wringing
his hands.*

NARRATOR:

So, when Shylock comes home he finds his daughter has
eloped, and with a Christian, and furthermore, has taken
all his gold and jewels . . .

Tubal enters and Shylock crosses anxiously to meet him.

NARRATOR:

. . . Tubal, a Hebrew friend, has gone in search of
Jessica, but though he often came where he did hear
of her, he could not find her. But he has other news.

Two-shot of Tubal and Shylock

TUBAL:

Other men have ill luck too: Antonio, as I heard in
Genoa,—

SHYLOCK:

What, what, what? ill luck, ill luck?

TUBAL:

—hath an argosy cast away, coming from Tripolis.

SHYLOCK:

I thank God, I thank God! Is't true, is't true?

TUBAL:

I spoke with some of the sailors that escaped the wreck.

SHYLOCK:

I thank thee, good Tubal: good news, good news! ha, ha! where? in Genoa?

TUBAL:

Your daughter spent in Genoa, as I heard, on one night, fourscore ducats.

SHYLOCK:

Thou stick'st a dagger in me: I shall never see my gold again: fourscore ducats at a sitting! fourscore ducats!

TUBAL:

There came divers of Antonio's creditors that swear he cannot choose but break.

SHYLOCK:

I am very glad of it: I'll plague him; I'll torture him: I am glad of it.

TUBAL:

One of them showed me a ring that he had of your daughter for a monkey.

SHYLOCK:

Out upon her! Thou torturest me, Tubal: it was my turquoise; I had it of Leah when I was a bachelor: I would not have given it for a wilderness of monkeys.

TUBAL:

But Antonio is certainly undone.

SHYLOCK:

Nay, that's true, that's very true. Go, Tubal, fee me an officer; bespeak him a fortnight before. I will have the heart of him, if he forfeit; for, were he out of Venice, I can make what merchandise I will. Go, go, Tubal, and meet me at our synagogue; go, good Tubal; at our synagogue, Tubal.

Dissolve to two-shot of Bassanio and Portia seated on a bench and regarding each other romantically. During the following narration they rise after a moment and stroll off upstage hand in hand. As they exeunt, Nerissa runs on laughing, pursued by Gratiano, also laughing. Catching her hand, Gratiano tries to get Nerissa to sit on the bench with him, but she pulls her hand free and runs off still laughing, and Gratiano follows her. Dissolve to medium shot of Shylock with his back to the audience and angrily shaking a clenched fist above his head.

NARRATOR:

So while Fortune favors Antonio's friends, his fortunes are disastrously reversed. The money borrowed from Shylock for Bassanio's amorous adventure will soon come due, and Shylock, angered by the abduction of his daughter and taunted by the crowds that jeer him in the streets will surely take revenge and take his pound of flesh. For when someone in the crowd cries, "I am sure thou wilt not take his flesh, what's that good for?", he turns to say . . .

Close on Shylock as he turns to face camera.

SHYLOCK:

To bait fish withal: if it will feed nothing else, it will feed my revenge. He hath disgraced me, and hindered me half a million; laughed at my losses, mocked at my gains, scorned my nation, thwarted my bargains, cooled my friends, heated mine enemies; and what's his reason? I am a Jew. Hath not a Jew eyes? hath not a Jew hands, organs, dimensions, senses, affections, passions? fed with the same food, hurt with the same weapons, subject to the same diseases, healed by the same means, warmed and cooled by the same winter and summer,

as a Christian is? If you prick us, do we not bleed? if
you tickle us, do we not laugh? if you poison us, do we
not die? and if you wrong us, shall we not revenge? if
we are like you in the rest, we will resemble you in that.
If a Jew wrong a Christian, what is his humility?
Revenge. If a Christian wrong a Jew, what should his
sufferance be by Christian example? Why, revenge. The
villainy you teach me, I will execute; and it shall go
hard but I will better the instruction.

*From close-up of Shylock dissolve slowly to close-up
of Portia.*

NARRATOR:

In Belmont, Lord Bassanio has won his love.

Dolly back to two-shot of Portia and Bassanio.

PORTIA:

You see me, Lord Bassanio, where I stand, such as I
am: myself and what is mine to you and yours is now
converted: This house, these servants, and this same
myself, are yours, my lord. I give them with this ring,
which when you part from, lose, or give away, let it
presage the ruin of your love, and be my vantage to
exclaim on you.

BASSANIO:

Madam, you have bereft me of all words,
Only my blood speaks to you in my veins;
But when this ring parts from this finger,
Then parts life from hence.

*Dolly to long shot including Portia and Bassanio and
Gratiano and Nerissa as they enter*

GRATIANO:

My Lord Bassanio and my gentle lady, I do beseech
you, that I may be married too.

BASSANIO:

With all my heart, so thou canst get a wife.

GRATIANO:

I thank your lordship, you have got me one.
My eyes, my lord, can look as swift as yours:
You saw the mistress, I beheld the maid.
Gratiano and Nerissa exchange happy glances.

PORTIA:

Is this true, Nerissa?

NERISSA:

Madam, it is, so you stand pleased withal.
*Camera close on Portia, who reacts to Bassanio's sudden
distress during the following narration.*

NARRATOR:

A day in April never came so sweet as does this happy
day for lovers, but joy is suddenly turned to dread as a
letter comes to Bassanio.

PORTIA:

With leave, Bassanio; I am half yourself,
And I must freely have the half of anything
That this same paper brings you.
*Two-shot of Portia and Bassanio. Bassanio is distressed
over the letter he holds in his hand.*

BASSANIO:

O sweet Portia, here are a few of the unpleasant'st
words that ever blotted paper! Gentle lady, I have
engaged myself to a dear friend, engaged my friend
to his mere enemy, to feed my means.
Bassanio reads from the letter.

BASSANIO:

My ships have all miscarried, my creditors grow cruel,
my estate is very low, my bond to the Jew is forfeit; and

since in paying it, it is impossible I should live, all debts are cleared between you and me, if I might but see you at my death.

PORTIA:

O love, dispatch all business, and be gone!

Long shot of Portia, Bassanio, Gratiano, and Nerissa. During the following narration, Gratiano and Bassanio bow to the girls and make their exit. Dissolve to long shot showing Antonio, Bassanio, and Gratiano entering a courtroom. In a moment the Duke enters and takes his position, then Shylock enters to stand before the Duke.

NARRATOR:

Learning of the nature of the trial, Portia persuades the judge, who is her uncle, to lend her judicial robes and let her go in his stead disguised as a learned doctor of the law, and with her, disguised as clerk, will go her maid, Nerissa. Now at the trial the Duke of Venice speaks:

DUKE:

Upon my power I may dismiss this court, unless Bellario, a learned doctor whom I have sent for to determine this, come here to-day.

SALERIO:

My lord, here stays without a messenger with letters from the doctor, new come from Padua.

DUKE:

Bring us the letters; call the messenger.

During the following narration letters are handed to the Duke, which he proceeds to study. In a moment Portia and Nerissa enter disguised as judge and court clerk. They are greeted by the Duke and Portia takes her position as judge, and Nerissa takes a position at the clerk's desk.

NARRATOR:
The Duke is much impressed with Bellario's recommendation of the young and learned judge and so the trial proceeds.

PORTIA:
Is your name Shylock?

SHYLOCK:
Shylock is my name.

PORTIA:
Of a strange nature is the suit you follow;
Yet in such rule that the Venetian law
Cannot impugn you as you do proceed.
You stand within his danger, do you not?

ANTONIO:
Ay, so he says.

PORTIA:
Do you confess the bond?

ANTONIO:
I do.

PORTIA:
Then must the Jew be merciful.

SHYLOCK:
On what compulsion must I? Tell me that.
Camera close on Portia

PORTIA:
The quality of mercy is not strain'd,
It droppeth as the gentle rain from heaven
Upon the place beneath: it is twice blest;
It blesseth him that gives, and him that takes:
'Tis mightiest in the mightiest: it becomes
The throned monarch better than his crown;
His sceptre shows the force of temporal power,
The attribute to awe and majesty,

Wherein doth sit the dread and fear of kings;
But mercy is above this sceptred sway;
It is enthroned in the hearts of kings,
It is an attribute to God himself;
And earthly power doth then show likest God's
When mercy seasons justice. Therefore, Jew,
Though justice be thy plea, consider this,
That, in the course of justice, none of us
Should see salvation: we do pray for mercy;
And that same prayer doth teach us all to render
The deeds of mercy.
Long shot including the entire court
I have spoke thus much
To mitigate the justice of thy plea;
Which if thou follow, this strict court of Venice
Must needs give sentence 'gainst the merchant there.

SHYLOCK:

My deeds upon my head! I crave the law,
The penalty and forfeit of my bond.

PORTIA:

Is he not able to discharge the money?

BASSANIO:

Yes, here I tender it for him in the court;
Yea, twice the sum. And I beseech you,
Wrest once the law to your authority:
To do a great right, do a little wrong,
And curb this cruel devil of his will.

RORTIA:

It must not be; there is no power in Venice
Can alter a decree established:
'Twill be recorded for a precedent,
And many an error, by the same example,
Will rush into the state: it cannot be.

SHYLOCK:

A Daniel come to judgment! yea, a Daniel!
O wise young judge, how I do honour thee!

PORTIA:

I pray you, let me look upon the bond.

Two-shot of Portia and Shylock

SHYLOCK:

Here 'tis, most reverend doctor, here it is.

PORTIA:

Shylock, there's thrice thy money offer'd thee.

SHYLOCK:

An oath, an oath, I have an oath in heaven.

PORTIA:

Why, this bond is forfeit;
And lawfully by this the Jew may claim
A pound of flesh, to be by him cut off
Nearest the merchant's heart. Be merciful:
Take thrice thy money; bid me tear the bond.

SHYLOCK:

When it is paid according to the tenour.
I stay here on my bond.

ANTONIO:

Most heartily I do beseech the court
To give the judgment.

PORTIA:

Why then, thus it is: you must prepare your bosom for
his knife.

SHYLOCK:

O noble Judge!

PORTIA:

Therefore, lay bare your bosom.

SHYLOCK:

Ay, his breast: nearest his heart.

PORTIA:

Have by some surgeon, Shylock, on your charge,
To stop his wounds, lest he do bleed to death.

SHYLOCK:

Is it so nominated in the bond? I cannot find it; 'tis not
in the bond.

Two-shot of Portia and Antonio

PORTIA:

You, merchant, have you any thing to say?

ANTONIO:

But little: I am arm'd and well prepared.

Two-shot of Antonio and Bassanio

Give me your hand, Bassanio: fare you well!
Repent but you that you shall lose your friend,
And he repents not that he pays your debt;
For if the Jew do cut but deep enough,
I'll pay it presently with all my heart.

Long shot of full court

SHYLOCK:

We trifle time: I pray thee, pursue sentence.

PORTIA:

A pound of that same merchant's flesh is thine:
The court awards it, and the law doth give it.

SHYLOCK:

Most rightful judge!

PORTIA:

And you must cut this flesh from off his breast:
The law allows it, and the court awards it.

SHYLOCK:

Most learned judge! A sentence! Come, prepare!

*Shylock moves in on Antonio and is about to cut his
breast when he is interrupted by Portia.*

PORTIA:

Tarry a little; there is something else.

This bond doth give thee here no jot of blood;
The words expressly are "a pound of flesh."
Take then thy bond, take thou thy pound of flesh;
But, in the cutting it, if thou dost shed
One drop of Christian blood, thy lands and goods
Are, by the laws of Venice, confiscate
Unto the state of Venice.

GRATIANO:

O upright judge! Mark, Jew: O learned judge!

SHYLOCK:

Is that the law?

PORTIA:

Thyself shalt see the act:
For, as thou urgest justice, be assured
Thou shalt have justice, more than thou desirest.

GRATIANO:

O learned judge! Mark, Jew: a learned judge!

SHYLOCK:

I take this offer, then; pay the bond thrice,
And let the Christian go.

BASSANIO:

Here is the money.

PORTIA:

Soft! The Jew shall have all justice; soft!,
no haste: he shall have nothing but the penalty.
Therefore, prepare thee to cut off the flesh.
Why doth the Jew pause? take thy forfeiture.

SHYLOCK:

Give me my principal, and let me go.

BASSANIO:

I have it ready for thee; here it is.

PORTIA:

He hath refused it in the open court:

He shall have merely justice and his bond.
GRATIANO:
A Daniel, still say I, a second Daniel!
I thank thee, Jew, for teaching me that word.
SHYLOCK:
Shall I not have barely my principal?
PORTIA:
Thou shalt have nothing but the forfeiture,
To be so taken at thy peril, Jew.
SHYLOCK:
Why, then the devil give him good of it.
I'll stay no longer question.
PORTIA:
Tarry, Jew:
The law hath yet another hold on you.
It is enacted in the laws of Venice,
If it be proved against an alien
That by direct or indirect attempts
He seek the life of any citizen,
The party 'gainst the which he doth contrive
Shall seize one half his goods; the other half
Comes to the privy coffer of the state;
And the offender's life lies in the mercy
Of the Duke only, 'gainst all other voice.
In which predicament, I say, thou stand'st;
Down, therefore, and beg mercy of the Duke.
DUKE:
That thou shalt see the difference of our spirits,
I pardon thee thy life before thou ask it.
PORTIA:
What mercy can you render him, Antonio?
Camera close on Antonio

ANTONIO:

So please my Lord the Duke and all the court
To quit the fine for one half of his goods,
I am content; so he will let me have
The other half in use, to render it,
Upon his death, unto the gentleman
That lately stole his daughter:
Two things provided more, that, for this favour,
He presently become a Christian;
The other, that he do record a gift,
Here in the court, of all he dies possess'd,
Unto his son Lorenzo and his daughter.

Camera close on Shylock

PORTIA:

Art thou contented, Jew? what dost thou say?

SHYLOCK:

I am content.

PORTIA:

Clerk, draw a deed of gift.

SHYLOCK:

I pray you, give me leave to go from hence;
I am not well.

*Long shot of full court. Shylock starts to leave, then
stops to look back at the judge.*

Send the deed after me, and I will sign it.

*Shylock leaves slowly as everyone else in the court
freezes to watch him. During the following narration
the Duke, Antonio, and Bassanio shake hands with
Portia. Then the Duke and Gratiano leave as the camera
closes in on Portia, Antonio, and Bassanio. The two men
try to persuade Portia to take money in payment for her
services. She refuses, then gets a mischievous idea.*

NARRATOR:

The lonely and defeated, yet not quite thoroughly defeated Shylock goes his way, and Bassanio and Antonio try in vain to reward the judge for justice. The judge persistently refuses, but the lady in the judge's robe then gets a mischievous idea.

Two-shot of Portia and Bassanio

PORTIA:

For your love, I'll take this ring from you.

BASSANIO:

This ring, good sir, alas, it is a trifle!
I will not shame myself to give you this.

PORTIA:

Well, peace be with you!

Portia strides off, followed by Nerissa. Bassanio looks after them in bewilderment. He is joined immediately by Gratiano and Antonio, who pleads in pantomime to have Bassanio give up the ring. Acquiescing, Bassanio hands the ring to Gratiano, indicating that he should run after the judge with it. Gratiano hurries off after the judge and clerk and Bassanio and Antonio exeunt in the opposite direction.

NARRATOR: *(during the above shot)*

But Antonio persuades Bassanio to give up the ring, and Gratiano hurries off with it to overtake the judge and clerk and Bassanio turns toward Belmont, taking his friend Antonio to meet his bride.

Two-shot of Lorenzo and Jessica seated romantically on a bench

And there, in the Belmont moonlight, awaiting the return of Portia and Nerissa, Lorenzo speaks amorously to his devoted Jessica.

LORENZO:

How sweet the moonlight sleeps upon this bank!
Here will we sit, and let the sounds of music

Creep in our ears. The man that hath no music
in himself, nor is not moved with concord of
sweet sounds, is fit for treasons, stratagems
and spoils. Let no such man be trusted.
*During the following narration dissolve to long shot
including Lorenzo, Jessica, Antonio, Bassanio, and
Portia and Nerissa, now dressed as themselves. Bassanio
introduces Antonio to Portia and the others. In a moment,
Gratiano and Nerissa enter arguing.*

NARRATOR:

Now all are home in Belmont and Bassanio presents his
friend Antonio to Portia and the others. All are home
and all should be well, but there is argument about . . .
Two-shot of Gratiano and Nerissa

GRATIANO:

A paltry ring that she did give me.

NERISSA:

You swore to me, when I did give it you,
That you would wear it till your hour of death.

GRATIANO:

My Lord Bassanio gave his ring away unto the judge
that begg'd it.
*Two-shot of Bassanio and Portia, who looks at him in
mock surprise*

PORTIA:

What ring gave you, my Lord?
Not that, I hope, which you received of me.
*Three-shot of Portia, Bassanio, and Antonio, who steps
in hoping to save the situation*

ANTONIO:

I once did lend my body for his wealth;
Which, but for him that had your husband's ring,
Had quite miscarried: I dare be bound again,

My soul upon the forfeit, that your lord
Will never more break faith advisedly.

PORTIA:

Then you shall be his surety. Give him this,
And bid him keep it better than the other.

ANTONIO:

Here, Lord Bassanio; swear to keep this ring.

BASSANIO:

By heaven, it is the same I gave the doctor!

PORTIA:

Here is a letter; read it at your leisure;
There you shall find that Portia was the doctor,
Nerissa there her clerk. Antonio, you are welcome;
And I have better news in store for you than you
expect: unseal this letter soon; There you shall
find three of your argosies are richly come to
harbour suddenly.

ANTONIO:

I am dumb.

Two-shot of Bassanio and Portia

BASSANIO:

Were you the doctor and I knew you not?
Sweet doctor, you shall be my bedfellow:
When I am absent, then lie with my wife.

*Long shot of entire group as Antonio finishes reading
his letter and smiles at Portia. Nerissa takes a document
to Lorenzo.*

NARRATOR:

The ring restored and Antonio's ships safely in port,
there are good comforts too for Lorenzo and his Jessica.

*Three-shot of Lorenzo, Jessica, and Nerissa as she hands
paper to Lorenzo*

NERISSA:
There do I give to you and Jessica,
From the rich Jew, a special deed of gift,
After his death, of all he dies possess'd of.

LORENZO:
Fair ladies, you drop manna in the way of starved people.
*Two-shot of Nerissa and Gratiano, who now regard
proudly Nerissa's ring, which is restored to his finger.*

Curtain

2

THE TAMING OF THE SHREW

The Taming of the Shrew

Synopsis

Often dubbed Shakespeare's funniest farce, *The Taming of the Shrew* is a raucous battle of wits, but it is a knock-down, drag-out battle too fast and furious for the witless. The witless, in this case, are the characters in the play who are baffled by the buffoonery of a temperamental, sharp-tongued young woman named Katherine and a cocky, high-spirited young man named Petruchio.

Katherine, or Kate, as swaggering Petruchio insists on calling her, is the eldest daughter of the rich Baptista, who is cowed by her and wants desperately to find a husband for her, offering a handsome dowry to any man who will take her off his hands. There are no takers. If there were, Katherine would scare them away with her tongue and temper. There are no takers until Petruchio comes to town.

Something of a fortune hunter and cocksure of his own good looks and masculinity, Petruchio learns about Katherine from an old friend named Hortensio, who is wooing Katherine's younger sister Bianca, a pampered Papa's darling who, according to custom, cannot marry until the eldest daughter is matrimonially disposed of. Hortensio's eagerness to see the older sister married so that his way will be cleared for a betrothal with Bianca prompts him to give Petruchio a warm description of Katherine. She is beautiful and she is rich, he tells Petruchio, but she

45

does have a temper and rails and scolds, he admits.

"Think you a little din can daunt mine ears?" says Petruchio, who is obviously impressed. Hortensio sees to it that Petruchio meets the father, Baptista, who, delighted at a prospective bridegroom, promptly sends Katherine to meet Petruchio.

They meet and immediately sparks fly between them. If they are sparks of ardor, and they are, Katherine is not about to let this cock of the walk know it is love at first sight. Her defense is up and the fight is on, she defiant and haughty, he resolute and masterful, and, though she kicks, bites, and scratches like a wildcat, Petruchio announces to her father when he reappears that they will be married on Sunday next.

Sunday comes but Petruchio does not. There is Katherine dressed for the wedding, but no bridegroom is in sight. She is in tears, tears of temper, when Petruchio sallies in, dressed like anything but a bridegroom.

"To me she's married, not unto my clothes," he says, and whisks her off to the church where, according to Grumio's account (Grumio being the mischievous man servant of Petruchio), Katherine is further humiliated by Petruchio's thoroughly unconventional antics.

Back at Baptista's house for the marriage feast, Petruchio shocks all present, including his bewildered bride, by swooping her up, tossing her over his shoulder, and heading for home before anyone has had a morsel of food.

In his home Petruchio is all kindness to his bride but it is a killing kind of kindness, which Katherine soon realizes is a game. Gently her husband removes each dish of food the servants bring to his hungry wife, then rails at the servants as he finds fault with the food, which he declares is not fit for a fine lady like his Katherine.

"This is a way to kill a wife with kindness," he says when she is out of the room. Pretending to be attentive to her every need, Petruchio will not let the mortified Katherine either eat or sleep, and, when she is so weary that she could drop in her tracks, he declares that they will journey to her father's house.

When they are nearly there, Petruchio chances to observe how brightly shines the moon. It is the sun, Katherine insists. "I say it is the moon," shouts Petruchio, and, pretending to be piqued at having his authority challenged, he announces that they will return to his house.

Ready to scream at the thought of having to trudge all that distance again, the bedraggled, befuddled Katherine suddenly sees light. Of course it is the moon, she admits, whereupon Petruchio perversely declares it is the sun. "Then God be bless'd, it is the blessed sun!" she says.

> "But sun it is not, when you say it is not,
> And the moon changes even as your mind:
> What you will have it nam'd, even that it is,
> And so it shall be so for Katherine."

Petruchio, amazed but pleased, puts her to one more test when he pretends that a passing old man is a fair young maiden, but Katherine, now grown wise, agrees that it is a maiden and plays the game to the hilt, much to the satisfaction of her husband.

Alive now to her husband's pranks of perversity, Katherine advises other women:

" . . . I am asham'd that women are so simple, to offer war, where they should kneel for peace, or seek for rule, supremacy and sway, when they are bound to serve, love and obey. . . . Place your hands below your husband's foot: in token of which duty, if he please, my hand is ready, may it do him ease."

But, when Petruchio places his foot in her hand, Katherine neatly trips him back on his haunches, proving that two can play at pranks, on which Petruchio grins and says, "Why there's a wench! Come on and kiss me Kate."

The Taming of the Shrew

(Video directions are in italics)

CAST

Narrator (who plays Baptista, Grumio, and Old Man)
Kate, a shrewish young woman
Her father, Baptista
Petruchio
Grumio
Old Man

> *Note:* The Narrator, who plays several of the
> incidental roles, should have the following in-
> serted before his first speech: "I am the nar-
> rator in this short version of the play, but in
> the telling of the tale I am actor, too, so you
> will see me first as one character, then another."

Kate chases Narrator as Baptista

KATE:

I pray you, sir, is it your will to make a stale of me
amongst these mates? If it were, doubt not my care
should be to comb your noodle with a three-legg'd stool,
and paint your face and use you like a fool! Why, and I
trust I may go too, may I not? What, shall I be appointed hours; as though, belike, I knew not what to take,
and what to leave, ha?

More chase

BAPTISTA:

Was ever gentleman grieved as I?

49

KATE:

Nay, father, chide me not, for I will marry no man till it please myself.

Kate exits

NARRATOR:

Katherine, Katherine—For shame, for shame.

Coming down

That's my daughter, Katherine. "The Shrew" they call her.

Petruchio is heard singing

And that's Petruchio. The play—"The Taming of the Shrew" by William Shakespeare. Yes, this is Shakespeare. Not Shakespeare in his *Hamlet* mood, or in a mood poetic or historic, but Shakespeare having fun, just unadulterated fun. Of course, we take some liberties with the text. We are a company of three. That means it falls to me to play an extra role or two. I am Baptista now, the father of the shrew, but if I doff my cape and change my hat, I can be Grumio, the zany servant to Petruchio, and with another presto change I'm suddenly Hortensio and he, you may recall, is Petruchio's old friend.

Petruchio enters

PETRUCHIO:

Verona, for a while I take my leave, to see my friends in Padua; but of all my best beloved and approved friend Hortensio, whose servant said I'd find him here. Here, sirrah Grumio, knock I say.

NARRATOR AS GRUMIO:

Knock sir? Whom should I knock? Is there any man has rebus'd your worship?

PETRUCHIO:

Villain I say, knock me here soundly.

NARRATOR:

Knock you here sir? Why sir, what am I sir, that I should knock you here sir?

PETRUCHIO:

Villain I say, knock me at this gate, and rap me well, or I'll knock your knave's pate.

NARRATOR:

My master is grown quarrelsome: I should knock you first, and then I know after who comes by the worst.

PETRUCHIO:

Will it not be? Faith, sirrah, and you'll not knock, I'll ring it, I'll try how you can sol, fa, and sing it.

He wrings him by the ears

NARRATOR:

Help, mistress, help: my master is mad.

PETRUCHIO:

Now knock when I bid you, sirrah villain.

NARRATOR:

Look you, if this be not a lawful cause for me to leave your service. You bid me knock you, and rap you soundly, sir.

PETRUCHIO:

You senseless villain—I bid you, rascal, knock upon the gate, and could not get you for my heart to do it.

NARRATOR:

Knock at the gate? Oh heavens, spake you not these words plain—"Sirrah, knock me here, rap me here, rap me well, and knock me soundly"? And come you now with knocking at the gate?

PETRUCHIO:

Sirrah, be gone, and talk not, I advise you. Go get you hence and bid my friend Hortensio attend me here. *Narrator exits*. I will await him with some tuneful idling.

He sings a lusty song

NARRATOR AS HORTENSIO: *(speaking off camera)*
How now, what's the matter? My old friend Grumio . . .
Narrator entering
. . . and my good friend Petruchio. How do you in
Verona?

PETRUCHIO:
Signior Hortensio.

NARRATOR:
But tell me now, sweet friend, what happy gale blows
you to Padua here, from old Verona?

PETRUCHIO:
Such wind as scatters young men through the world to
seek their fortunes farther than at home, where small
experience grows. But in a few, Signior Hortensio, thus
it stands with me: Antonio my father is deceased, and I
have thrust myself into this maze, haply to wive and
thrive, as best I may: Crowns in my purse I have, and
goods at home, and so am come abroad to see the world.

NARRATOR:
I can, Petruchio, help thee to a wife
With wealth enough, and young and beauteous,
Brought up as best becomes a gentlewoman.
Her only fault, and that is faults enough,
Is that she is intolerable curst,
And shrewd, and froward, so beyond all measure
That were my state far worser than it is,
I would not wed her for a mine of gold.

PETRUCHIO:
Hortensio, peace: thou know'st not gold's effect,
Tell me her father's name, and tis enough:
For I will board her, though she chide as loud
as Thunder, when the clouds in autumn crack.

NARRATOR:
Her father is Baptista Minola,
An affable and courteous gentleman,
Her name is Katherina Minola,
Renown'd in Padua for her scolding tongue.

PETRUCHIO:
I know her father, though I know not her,
And he knew my deceased father well.
I will not sleep, Hortensio, till I see her.

NARRATOR:
Well, wait here, my friend, and I will send
her father forth, that you may speak with him.

PETRUCHIO:
Do so, I pray.
Narrator exits

KATE: *(off camera)*
Talk not to me. I will go sit and weep until I can find
occasion for revenge.
*Kate enters; they look at one another, establishing a fiery
love at first sight. She kicks Petruchio and leaves.*
Narrator reenters as Baptista

NARRATOR:
God save you, gentle sir.
They sit

PETRUCHIO:
And you, good sir: pray have you not a daughter call'd
Katherine, fair and virtuous?

NARRATOR:
I have a daughter, sir, call'd Katherine.

PETRUCHIO:
I am a gentleman of Verona, sir,
That hearing of her beauty, and her wit,
Her affability and bashful modesty:
Her wondrous qualities, and mild behaviour,

Am bold to show myself a forward guest
Within your house.

NARRATOR:
You're welcome sir.
But for my daughter, Katherine, this I know,
She is not for your turn, the more my grief.

PETRUCHIO: *Stands*
I see you do not mean to part with her,
Or else you like not of my company.

NARRATOR:
Mistake me not, I speak but as I find,
Whence are you, sir? What may I call your name?

PETRUCHIO:
Petruchio is my name, Antonio's son,
A man well known throughout all Italy.

NARRATOR:
I know him well, Signior Petruchio. Will you go with me
or shall I send my daughter Kate to you?

PETRUCHIO:
I pray you do.
Narrator exits
Kate yells
I will attend her here,
And woo her with some spirit when she comes.
But here she comes, and now Petruchio, speak.
Enter Kate from camera right
Good morrow, Kate, for that's your name I hear.

KATE:
Well have you heard, but something hard of hearing.
They call me Katherine, that do talk of me.

PETRUCHIO:
You lie in faith, for you are called plain Kate,
And bonny Kate, and sometimes Kate the curst:

But Kate, the prettiest Kate in Christendom,
Kate of Kate-Hall, my super-dainty Kate,
For dainties are all cates, and therefore Kate,
Take this of me, Kate of my consolation,
Hearing thy mildness prais'd in every town,
Thy virtue spoke of, and thy beauty sounded,
Yet not so deeply as to thee belongs,
Myself am mov'd to woo thee for my wife.

Kate to center

KATE:

Mov'd in good time, let him that mov'd you hither
Remove you hence: I knew you at the first you were
a moveable.

PETRUCHIO:

Why, what's a moveable?

KATE:

A join'd stool.

PETRUCHIO:

Thou hast hit it; come sit on me.

KATE:

Asses are made to bear, and so are you.

PETRUCHIO:

Women are made to bear, and so are you.

KATE:

No such jade as you, if me you mean.

PETRUCHIO:

Alas good Kate, I will not burthen thee,
For knowing thee to be but young and light.

KATE:

Too light for such a swain as you to catch,
And yet as heavy as my weight should be.

PETRUCHIO:

Should be, should: buzz.

KATE:

Well ta'en, and like a buzzard.

PETRUCHIO:

O slow-winged turtle, shall a buzzard take thee?

KATE:

Ay, for a turtle, as he takes a buzzard.

PETRUCHIO:

Come, come, you wasp, i' faith you are too angry.

KATE:

If I be waspish, best beware my sting.

PETRUCHIO:

My remedy is then to pluck it out.

KATE:

Ay, if the fool could find it where it lies.

PETRUCHIO:

Who knows not where a wasp does wear his sting? In his tail.

KATE:

In his tongue!

PETRUCHIO:

Whose tongue?

KATE:

Yours if you talk of tales, and so farewell.

PETRUCHIO:

What! With my tongue in your tail?
Nay, come again, good Kate, I am a gentleman.
Kate, you must not look so sour.

KATE:

It is my fashion when I see a crab.

PETRUCHIO:

Why? here's no crab, and therefore look not sour.

KATE:

There is, there is.

PETRUCHIO:
Then show it me.

KATE:
Had I a glass, I would.

PETRUCHIO:
What, you mean my face?

KATE:
Well aim'd of such a young one.

PETRUCHIO:
Now, by Saint George, I am too young for you.

KATE:
Yet, you are wither'd.

PETRUCHIO:
Tis with cares.

KATE:
I care not.

PETRUCHIO:
Nay, hear you, Kate. In sooth you 'scape not so.

As Kate starts to leave, he grabs her and they struggle

KATE:
I chafe you if I tarry. Let me go.

PETRUCHIO:
No, not a whit, I find you passing gentle:
It was told me you were rough, and coy, and sullen,
And now I find report a very liar:
For thou art pleasant, gamesome, passing courteous,
But slow in speech: yet sweet as spring-time flowers,
Thou canst not frown, thou canst not look askance,
Nor bite the lip as angry wenches will,
Nor hast thou pleasure to be cross in talk,
But thou with mildness entertain'st thy wooers,
With gentle conference, soft, and affable.

Why does the world report that Kate doth limp?
Oh let me see thee walk: thou dost not halt.

KATE:

Go, fool, and whom thou keep'st command.

PETRUCHIO:

Did ever Dian so become a grove
As Kate this chamber with her princely gait:
O be thou Dian, and let her be Kate,
And then let Kate be chaste, and Dian sportful.

KATE:

Where did you study all this goodly speech?

PETRUCHIO:

It is extempore, from the mother wit.

KATE:

A witty mother, witless else her son.

PETRUCHIO:

Am I not wise?

KATE:

Yes, keep you warm.

PETRUCHIO:

Marry so I mean, sweet Katherine, in thy bed:
And therefore setting all this chat aside,
Thus in plain terms: your father hath consented
That you shall be my wife; your dowry 'greed on,
And will you, nill you, I will marry you.
Petruchio kisses Kate
Enter Narrator as Baptista

NARRATOR:

Now, Signior Petruchio, how speed you with my
daughter?

PETRUCHIO:

How but well, sir? How but well?
It were impossible I should speed amiss.

NARRATOR:

Why how now daughter Katherine, in your dumps?

KATE:

Call you me daughter? Now I promise you
You have showed a tender fatherly regard,
To wish me wed to one half lunatic
A mad-cap ruffian, and swearing jack,
That thinks with oaths to face the matter out.

PETRUCHIO:

Father, 'tis thus, yourself and all the world
That talk'd of her, have talk'd amiss of her:
And to conclude, we have 'greed so well together,
That upon Sunday is the wedding day.

KATE:

I'll see thee hang'd on Sunday first.

NARRATOR:

Hark Petruchio, she says she'll see thee hang'd first.

PETRUCHIO:

Be patient, father. I choose her for myself.
If she and I be pleased, what's that to you?
'Tis bargain'd 'twixt us twain being alone,
That she shall still be curst in company.
I tell you 'tis incredible to believe
How much she loves me: oh the kindest Kate,
She hung about my neck, and kiss on kiss
She vied so fast, protesting oath on oath
That in a twink she won me to her love.
Give me thy hand, Kate.
Kate swings, hitting Narrator by mistake.

NARRATOR:

I know not what to say, but give me your hands.

PETRUCHIO:

I will unto Venice to buy apparel 'gainst the wedding

day; provide the feast, father, and bid the guests, I will
be sure my Katherine shall be fine.

NARRATOR:

God send you joy, Petruchio! 'tis a match.

PETRUCHIO:

We will be married 'a Sunday!

Kate stamps foot, exits

Petruchio exits

NARRATOR:

Till Sunday next, adieu to you, Petruchio,
my son, my future in-law son. Oh, fortune,
fortune, now let Sunday come apace.

Black and up—fast

Anon 'tis near. Anon 'tis here. This is
the appointed day when Katherine and Petruchio
should be married, and yet we hear not of our
son-in-law. What will be said? What mockery
will it be to want the bridegroom when the
feast is hence to seek the ceremonial rites of
marriage.

Kate enters

What say you, daughter, to this shame of ours?

KATE:

No shame but mine, I must forsooth be forc'd
to give my hand oppos'd against my heart
Unto a mad-brain rudesby, full of spleen,
Who woo'd in haste, and means to wed at leisure;
He'll woo a thousand, 'point the day of marriage,
Make friends, invite, and proclaim the banns,
Yet never means to wed where he hath woo'd.

Enter Petruchio in outlandish cape and hat

Kate exits

PETRUCHIO:

Come, where be these gallants? Who's at home?

NARRATOR:

You are welcome sir.

PETRUCHIO:

And yet I come not well.

NARRATOR:

Not so well apparell'd as I wish you were. Why sir, you know this is your wedding day.

PETRUCHIO:

Where is Kate? I stay too long from her,
The morning wears, 'tis time we were at Church.

NARRATOR:

See not your bride in these unreverent robes.
Come to my chamber. Put on clothes of mine.

PETRUCHIO:

Not I, believe me. Thus I'll visit her.

NARRATOR:

But thus I trust you will not marry her.

PETRUCHIO:

Good sooth, even thus.

Narrator shakes his head and exits

PETRUCHIO: *(to camera)*

Therefore have done with words.
To me she's married, not unto my clothes.
But what a fool am I to chat with you,
When I should bid good morrow to my bride,
And seal the title with a lovely kiss.

Petruchio exits

Narrator as Grumio enters from camera right

NARRATOR:

Oh, haste me, haste me from the church. What a wedding, what a bridegroom, what a bride. Why she's a devil and he's a devil, a very fiend! Oh, she's a devil, a devil's dam, but she's a lamb, a dove, compared to him. When the priest did ask if Katherine should be his bride, Ah, by God's wounds, quothed he, and swore so loud that, all amazed, the priest let fall the book. And as he stooped to pick it up the mad brained bridegroom gave him such a cuff that down fell book and priest and priest and book. And he, the bridegroom, stomped and swore as if the vicar meant to cousin him. This done, he took the bride about the neck and kissed her lips with such a clamorous smack that, at the parting, all the church did echo! And I, seeing this, came thence for very shame, and after me I know the rout is coming. Such a mad marriage never was before.

Narrator exits

Petruchio enters dragging a bedraggled Kate

PETRUCHIO:

Gentlemen and friends, I thank you for your
pains. I know you think to dine with me today,

She tries to get away

And have prepar'd great store of wedding cheer,
But so it is, my haste doth call me hence,
And therefore here I mean to take my leave.

Narrator as Baptista enters

NARRATOR:

Is't possible you will away tonight?

PETRUCHIO:

I must away today, before night come,
Make it no wonder: if you knew my business,
You would entreat me rather go than stay:
And honest company, I thank you all,
That have beheld me give away myself
To this most patient, sweet, and virtuous wife.

Dine with my father, drink a health to me,
For I must hence, and farewell to you all.

NARRATOR:

Let us entreat you stay till after dinner.

PETRUCHIO:

It may not be.

NARRATOR: *(as Grumio)*

Let me entreat you.

PETRUCHIO:

It cannot be.

KATE:

Let me entreat you.

Narrator exits

PETRUCHIO:

I am content.

KATE:

Are you content to stay?

PETRUCHIO:

I am content you shall entreat me stay,
But yet not stay, entreat me how you can.

KATE:

Now, if you love me, stay.

Narrator as Grumio enters

PETRUCHIO:

Grumio, my horse.

NARRATOR:

Ay sir, they be ready, the oats have eaten the horses!
Oooooooh!

Narrator exits

KATE:

Nay then,
Say what thou canst, I will not go today,
No, nor tomorrow, not till I please myself.

The door is open sir, there lies your way;
You may be jogging whiles your boots are green:
For me, I'll not be gone till I please myself.
'Tis like you'll prove a jolly surly groom
That take it on you at the first so roundly.

PETRUCHIO:

O Kate, content thee, prithee be not angry.

KATE:

I will be angry, what hast thou to do?
He shall stay my leisure.
Gentlemen, forward to the bridal dinner,
I see a woman may be made a fool
If she has not a spirit to resist.

PETRUCHIO:

They shall go forward, Kate, at thy command,
Obey the bride, you that attend on her,
Go to the feast, revel and domineer,
Carouse full measure to her maidenhead,
Be mad and merry, or go hang yourselves:
But for my bonny Kate, she must with me.
She is my goods, my chattels, she is my house,
My household stuff, my field, my barn,
My horse, my ox, my ass, my anything.
Grumio, draw forth thy weapon. We're beset
with thieves, rescue thy mistress if thou be a
man: Fear not, sweet wench, they shall not
touch thee, Kate, I'll buckler thee against
a million.

Petruchio and Kate exit left
End of scene. Black
Up on: Petruchio's house. Narrator as Grumio under
table

PETRUCHIO: *(off camera)*

Grumio, You beetle-nosed clunkhead.

NARRATOR:

Cock's passion. Here they are.

Petruchio and Kate enter left

PETRUCHIO:

Where be that knave? No man at door to hold my stirrup or to take my horse? Where is the foolish knave I sent before?

NARRATOR:

Here sir, as foolish as I was before.

Petruchio pulls Narrator up by the hair

PETRUCHIO:

You peasant swain, you whoreson malt-horse drudge, Did I not bid thee meet me in the park? Go rascal, go, and fetch my supper in.

Narrator exits

Where is the life that late I led?

Where are those? Sit down Kate, and welcome.

Narrator as Grumio enters

Food, food, food, food. Why when, I say?

Nay, good sweet Kate, be merry.

Off with my boots, you rogue, you villain, when?

Narrator pulls boots and exits.

Narrator enters with food

What's this, mutton?

NARRATOR:

Aye.

PETRUCHIO:

Who brought it?

NARRATOR:

I.

PETRUCHIO:

'Tis burnt, and so is all the meat:

What dogs are these?
How durst you, villain, bring it from the
dresser and serve it thus to me that love
it not? There, take it to you, trenchers,
cups, and all: You heedless jolthead, and
unmanner'd slave.
Narrator exits camera right
KATE:
I pray you, husband, be not so disquiet,
The meat was well, if you were so contented.
PETRUCHIO:
I tell thee Kate, 'twas burnt and dried away,
And I expressly am forbid to touch it.
Be patient, tomorrow it shall be mended,
And for this night we'll fast for company.
Go, I will join thee in thy bridal chamber.
Exit Kate camera left
Thus have I politicly begun my reign,
And 'tis my hope to end successfully.
For this is a way to kill a wife with kindness,
He that knows better how to tame a shrew,
Now let him speak, 'tis charity to show.
Exit Petruchio camera left
Kate enters camera left
Narrator as Grumio enters camera right
KATE:
The more my wrong, the more his spite appears.
What, did he marry me to famish me?
I'm starv'd for meat, giddy for lack of sleep:
With oaths kept waking, and with brawling fed,
And that which spites me more than all these wants,
He does it under name of perfect love:

I prithee go, and get me some repast,
I care not what, so it be wholesome food.

NARRATOR:

What say you to a neat's foot?

KATE:

'Tis passing good, I prithee let me have it.

NARRATOR:

I fear it is too choleric a meat.
How say you to a fat tripe finely broil'd?

KATE:

I like it well, good Grumio, fetch it me.
He sits at her feet

NARRATOR:

I cannot tell, I fear 'tis choleric.
What say you to a piece of beef and mustard?

KATE:

A dish that I do love to feed upon.

NARRATOR:

Ay, but the mustard is too hot a little.

KATE:

Why then the beef, and let the mustard rest.

NARRATOR:

Nay, then I will not, you shall have the mustard or else
you get no beef of Grumio.

KATE:

Then both or one, or anything you wilt.

NARRATOR:

Why then the mustard without the beef.

KATE:

Go get thee gone, thou false deluding slave . . .
She beats him
that feed'st me with the very name of meat.

Enter Petruchio camera left, holding plate of meat behind him. Grumio exits camera left.

PETRUCHIO:

How fares my Kate, what sweeting, all amort?

KATE:

Faith, as cold as can be.

PETRUCHIO:

Pluck up thy spirits, look cheerfully upon me.

Here, love, thou seest how diligent I am,

To dress thy meat myself, and bring it thee.

Kate sits. Petruchio puts meat in front of her, then pulls it away.

PETRUCHIO:

I am sure, sweet Kate, this kindness merits thanks:

What, not a word? Nay, then, thou lov'st it not:

And all my pains is sorted to no proof.

Here, Grumio, take away this dish.

KATE:

I pray you let it stand.

PETRUCHIO:

The poorest service is repaid with thanks,

And so shall mine before you touch the meat.

KATE:

I thank you sir.

PETRUCHIO:

Kate eat apace . . . what, has thou dined?

Petruchio replaces meat only to remove it immediately. Narrator as Grumio enters camera left, takes meat, exits camera left.

. . . and now my honey love, we will return unto thy father's house, and revel it as bravely as the best; Grumio, go call my men and bring our horses unto Long-Lane end, there will we mount, and thither walk on foot; Let's see, I think 'tis now some seven o'clock, and well we may come there by dinner time.

KATE:

I dare assure you sir, 'tis almost two, and 'twill be supper time ere you come there.

PETRUCHIO:

It shall be seven ere I go to horse:
Look, what I speak or do, or think to do,
You are still crossing it! Sirs, let 't alone,
I will not go today, and ere I do,
It shall be what o'clock I say it is.

Petruchio is sitting on edge of table, back to Kate. They steal looks at each other, then Kate picks up boots and starts putting them on Petruchio. Petruchio smiles smugly. Kate reacts by slamming boot to floor and stalking off. End of scene. Black.

Up on Narrator, on road

NARRATOR:

They're off, off to her father's house. But on the way there's still a bit of taming yet to do. We're not quite through with Taming of the Shrew.

Black, Narrator as Grumio walks into picture of Petruchio and Kate on road.

PETRUCHIO:

Come on, 'a God's name, once more toward our father's house. Good Lord, how bright and goodly shines the moon.

KATE:

The moon, the sun! It is not moonlight now.

PETRUCHIO:

I say it is the moon that shines so bright.

KATE:

I know it is the sun that shines so bright.

PETRUCHIO:

Now by my mother's son, and that's myself,
It shall be moon, or star, or what I list,
Or ere I journey to your father's house!
Go on, and fetch our horses back again,
Evermore cross'd and cross'd, nothing but cross'd.

NARRATOR:

Say as he says, or we shall never go.
*Kate throws tantrum, which Petruchio ignores, then
makes decision to try another tactic.*

KATE:

Forward I pray, since we have come so far,
And be it moon, or sun, or what you please:
And if you please to call it a rush candle,
Henceforth I vow it shall be so for me!

PETRUCHIO:

I say it is the moon.

KATE:

I know it is the moon.

PETRUCHIO:

Nay then you lie: it is the blessed sun.

KATE:

Then God be bless'd, it is the blessed sun!
But sun it is not, when you say it is not,
And the moon changes even as your mind:
What you will have it nam'd, even that it is,
And so it shall be so for Katherine.

PETRUCHIO:

Well, forward, forward, thus the bowl should run,
And not unluckily against the bias:
But soft, what company is coming here?
Narrator as old man enters
Camera left

Good morrow, gentle Mistress, where away?
Tell me sweet Kate, and tell me truly too,
Hast thou beheld a fresher gentlewoman?
Sweet Kate embrace her for her beauty's sake.

KATE:
Young budding virgin, fair, and fresh, and sweet,
Whither away, or whither is thy abode?
Happy the parents of so fair a child;
Happier the man who favourable stars
Allot thee for his lovely bedfellow.

PETRUCHIO:
Why, how now Kate, I hope thou art not mad,
This is a man, old, wrinkled, faded, withered,
And not a maiden, as thou sayest he is.

KATE:
Pardon, old father, my mistaking eyes,
That have been so bedazzled with the sun,
That everything I look on seemeth green.
Narrator exits camera right

PETRUCHIO:
Katherine, that cap becomes you not.
Off with that bauble, throw it under foot.
Narrator as Grumio enters
Katherine, I charge thee, tell these headstrong women
what duty they do owe their lords and husbands.

KATE:
Thy husband is thy lord, thy life, thy keeper, thy head,
thy sovereign: one that cares for thee, and for thy
maintenance. I am asham'd that women are so simple,
to offer war, where they should kneel for peace, or seek
for rule, supremacy and sway, when they are bound to
serve, love and obey. Come, come, you froward and
unable worms, my mind hath been as big as one of yours,

my heart as great, my reason haply more, to bandy word for word, and frown for frown: But now I see our lances are but straws: our strength as weak, our weakness past compare, that seeming to be most, which we indeed least are, then vail your stomachs, for it is no boot, and place your hands below your husband's foot: in token of which duty, if he please, my hand is ready, may it do him ease.

Kate kneels, places hand for Petruchio's foot, then upsets him. He rises, laughs

PETRUCHIO:

Why there's a wench! Come on, and kiss me, Kate!

Kisses Kate and all three grin at camera

Black

Curtain

3
ROMEO AND JULIET

Romeo and Juliet

Synopsis

Neighbors who hate each other often bring sorrow on themselves and others, but true love can win over hatred and even triumph over death. A girl named Juliet Capulet had a neighbor named Romeo Montague, but the two had never met because their families hated each other. The hatred was so bitter that the Capulets took pains to see that no Montagues ever came to their parties. In Shakespeare's play it all took place in Verona, Italy, a long time ago, but it could happen any time, any place, especially where there are hateful neighbors who are overly strict with their children.

In the play the Capulets are giving a dance, a kind of coming-out party, for their only daughter, Juliet, and it is hoped by her parents that she will meet and agree to marry a proper young man named Paris, Papa's choice for his darling. News of the affair spreads up and down the street, and the venturesome young Romeo, along with his friend Mercutio and other cronies, decides to crash the party, not too difficult a feat, since all of the guests are invited to come in masquerade.

At the ball Romeo and Juliet meet and engage in a charming repartee. Not until they have fallen deeply in love do they learn each other's identity and that they are mortal enemies because of their families' feud.

Who was that fascinating young man, Juliet asks of her old nurse as Romeo is leaving. "Romeo," says the

75

nurse, horrified, "and a Montague." A Montague in the house of the Capulets? Scandalous. The scandalous intrusion has not been unnoticed by Tybalt, Juliet's fiery young cousin, who is something of a hothead. He will get even, he tells Juliet's father.

Later that night Juliet steps out on her balcony to talk to herself about her overwhelming feeling for this Romeo, a Montague. Romeo, determined to catch another glimpse of the girl he has fallen in love with, risks death by the Capulet clan to scale a wall and drop into the garden, where he sees his dream girl, beautiful in the moonlight. Overhearing her admit her love for him, Romeo climbs to the balcony. Some of the greatest love poetry in the world is interrupted by the old nurse's calling Juliet to come to bed. Juliet goes inside, but reappears to ask Romeo if his intent is to marry her. It is indeed, and they get married the next day in the monastic cell of Romeo's friend and Juliet's confessor, Friar Laurence. The old Friar is glad enough to marry them, in the hope that such a union will bring about amity between the Capulets and the Montagues. Unfortunately, it does not work out that way.

Some time after the secret marriage, there is a street brawl in which Romeo's best friend, Mercutio, is killed by the fiery cousin Tybalt. Romeo is so shocked and grieved by his friend's death that he fences with Tybalt and kills the cousin of his bride. For this rash deed, Romeo is banished by the Duke.

Hearing of this, Juliet is torn between loyalty to her cousin and love for her bridegroom, but knows in her heart that she must see Romeo again before he is banished. She sends her faithful nurse to find him.

In the wee hours before dawn, Romeo risks his life

again, to join Juliet in her boudoir, knowing that he must be out of the city by daybreak or face death by order of the Duke.

In their moment of heaven together it is not the lark that is singing, Juliet insists, but the nightingale, but the first streak of eastern light convinces them both that it is indeed the lark, so they say a painful farewell, swearing they will still manage to get together somehow.

Knowing nothing of Juliet's marriage to Romeo, Papa Capulet decides he will marry off his daughter at once to young Paris, and is even more insistent when he discovers his daughter's stubborn reluctance in the matter.

Desperate, and determined not to marry Paris, Juliet seeks the advice and aid of friend Friar Laurence, who, after some hesitation, gives her a sleeping potion which, when she drinks it, will make her appear dead for several hours. Back in her room she drinks the potion and, when the nurse comes to waken her for her nuptials with Paris, is presumably dead.

Grief-stricken, the unknowing Capulets have her borne to the family tomb, where the friar, by previous understanding with Juliet, is to come and secretly spirit her away to Mantua where Romeo is. Unfortunately, news of the plot fails to reach Romeo and instead he hears the awful news that Juliet has died and been taken to the Capulet tomb. Desperate with grief, Romeo buys some poison and returns to the Capulet tomb, determined to end his life beside his beloved. He does so just as Friar Laurence arrives, expecting to waken Juliet and secretly escort her to her Romeo. Instead, he finds Romeo dead beside her. Fleeing for help, he dashes out of the tomb, leaving Juliet to face the reality of her young husband's death alone. Unable to bear the thought of living without her Romeo, she stabs herself and dies, falling across Romeo's body.

Friar Laurence returns and with him are the fathers of both bride and bridegroom, along with the Duke and others. Seeing the horror their hatred has wrought, and admonished by the Duke, the two fathers shake hands as their hatred melts in sorrow. As they vow their eternal friendship, the Duke says:

> "Never was a story of more woe,
> Than this of Juliet and her Romeo."

Romeo and Juliet

(Video directions are in italics)

CAST

Narrator	Juliet
Lady Capulet,	Romeo
Juliet's mother	Friar Laurence
Nurse	Capulet, Juliet's father

Note: The roles of Friar Laurence and Capulet may be played by the Narrator, in which case the following should be added to the opening speech: "I shall also appear as Friar Laurence and as Capulet. I pray you know me when we meet."

Close on Narrator

NARRATOR:

Two households both alike in dignity,
(In fair Verona where we lay our scene)
From ancient grudge, break to new mutiny,
Where civil blood makes civil hands unclean:
From forth the fatal loins of these two foes,
A pair of star-cross'd lovers, take their life:
Whose misadventur'd piteous overthrows,
Doth with their death bury their parents' strife.
So speaks the Prologue to the Tragedy of Romeo and Juliet by William Shakespeare. And in this vignette version, I, as Prologue, narrate the play.

Three-shot of Juliet, Nurse, and Lady Capulet

LADY CAPULET:

Nurse, where's my daughter? Call her forth to me.

NURSE:

What Juliet.

Enter Juliet

JULIET:

How now who calls?

NURSE:

Your mother.

JULIET:

Madam I am here, what is your will?

LADY CAPULET:

This is the matter. Thou knowest my daughter's of a pretty age.

NURSE:

Faith I can tell her age unto an hour.

Thou wast the prettiest babe that e'er I nurs'd,

And I might live to see thee married once,

I have my wish.

LADY CAPULET:

Marry, that marry is the very theme

I came to talk of, tell me daughter Juliet,

How stands your disposition to be married?

JULIET:

It is an honour that I dream not of.

LADY CAPULET:

Well think of marriage now;

The valiant Paris seeks you for his love.

What say you, can you love the gentleman?

This night you shall behold him at our feast.

Speak briefly, can you like of Paris' love?

JULIET:

I'll look to like, if looking liking move.

But no more deep will I endart mine eye,
Than your consent gives strength to make it fly.
Close on Narrator
NARRATOR:
Not Paris, though, but Romeo is fair Juliet's choice when
first they meet. But he is of the house of Montague, and
she a Capulet. And ancient is the hate these families bear,
one for the other.
Two-shot of Romeo and Juliet
ROMEO:
If I profane with my unworthiest hand,
This holy shrine, the gentle sin is this,
My lips two blushing Pilgrims ready stand,
To smooth the rough touch with a gentle kiss.
Romeo takes Juliet's hand, kisses it.
JULIET:
Good Pilgrim, you do wrong your hand too much
With mannerly devotion shows in this,
For saints have hands, that Pilgrims' hands do touch,
And palm to palm is holy Palmers' kiss.
ROMEO:
Have not saints lips and holy Palmers too?
JULIET:
Ay Pilgrim, lips that they must use in prayer.
ROMEO:
O then dear Saint, let lips do what hands do,
They pray, grant thou, lest faith turn to despair.
JULIET:
Saints do not move, though grant for prayers' sake.
ROMEO:
Then move not while my prayer's effect I take,
Thus from my lips, by thine my sin is purg'd.
Romeo kisses Juliet

JULIET:

Then have my lips the sin that they have took.

ROMEO:

Sin from my lips, O trespass sweetly urg'd:
Give me my sin again.

He kisses her again

JULIET:

You kiss by th' book.

Camera spreads to catch Nurse as she enters

NURSE:

Madam your mother craves a word with you.

ROMEO:

What is her mother?

NURSE:

Marry bachelor,
Her mother is the Lady of the house.

ROMEO:

Is she a Capulet?
O dear account! my life is my foe's debt.

Romeo moves off camera

JULIET:

Come hither Nurse, what is yon gentleman?

NURSE:

His name is Romeo, and a Montague,
The only son of your great enemy.

Close on Juliet

JULIET:

My only love sprung from my only hate.

Close on Narrator

NARRATOR:

Now, in the night, to the Capulet garden Romeo returns.

Two-shot of Romeo and Juliet, using balcony. Romeo

*stands below balcony. Juliet stands on balcony, looking
away from Romeo.*

ROMEO:

Soft now, what light through yonder window breaks?
It is the East, and Juliet is the Sun.
See how she leans her cheek upon her hand,
That I might touch that cheek.

JULIET:

Ay me.

ROMEO:

She speaks. Oh speak again, bright Angel.

JULIET:

O Romeo, Romeo, wherefore art thou Romeo?
Deny thy father and refuse thy name.
Or if thou wilt not, be but sworn my love,
And I'll no longer be a Capulet.

ROMEO:

Shall I hear more, or shall I speak at this?

JULIET:

'Tis but thy name that is mine enemy:
Thou art thyself, though not a Montague,
What's Montague? It is nor hand nor foot,
Nor arm nor face, nor any other part
Belonging to a man. O be some other name.
What's in a name? That which we call a rose,
By any other name would smell as sweet,
So Romeo would were he not Romeo call'd,
Retain that dear perfection which he owes,
Without that title. Romeo doff thy name,
And for thy name which is not part of thee,
Take all my self.

ROMEO:

I take thee at thy word:
Call me but love, and I'll be new baptiz'd,
Henceforth I never will be Romeo.

JULIET: *(looking at Romeo)*

What man art thou, that thus bescreen'd in night
So stumblest on my counsel?

ROMEO:

By a name,
I know not how to tell thee who I am:
My name dear saint, is hateful to myself,
Because it is an enemy to thee.

JULIET:

My ears have not yet drunk a hundred words
Of thy tongue's utterance, yet I know the sound.
Art thou not Romeo, and a Montague?

ROMEO:

Neither fair maid, if either thee dislike.

JULIET:

How cam'st thou hither, tell me, and wherefore?
The orchard walls are high and hard to climb,
And the place death, considering who thou art,
If any of my kinsmen find thee here.

ROMEO:

With love's light wings did I o'er-perch these walls,
For stony limits cannot hold love out.
Lady, by yonder blessed Moon I swear,
That tips with silver all these fruit-tree tops . . .

JULIET:

O swear not by the Moon, the inconstant Moon.

ROMEO:

What shall I swear by?

JULIET:

Do not swear at all:

Or if thou wilt, swear by thy gracious self,
Which is the god of my idolatry,
And I'll believe thee.
My bounty is as boundless as the sea,
My love as deep, the more I give to thee
The more I have, for both are infinite.
NURSE: *(off camera)*
Madam!
JULIET:
Anon, good Nurse.
ROMEO:
O blessed blessed night, I am afeard
Being in night, all this is but a dream,
Too flattering-sweet to be substantial.
JULIET:
Three words dear Romeo, and good night indeed:
If that thy bent of love be honourable,
Thy purpose marriage, send me word to-morrow,
By one that I'll procure to come to thee,
Where and what time thou wilt perform the rite,
And all my fortunes at thy feet I'll lay,
And follow thee my Lord throughout the world.
NURSE: *(off camera)*
Madam!
JULIET:
I come, anon. A thousand times good night.
Juliet goes off camera
ROMEO:
A thousand times the worse to want thy light.
Juliet reappears
JULIET:
Romeo.

ROMEO:

My dear.

JULIET:

I have forgot why I did call thee back.

ROMEO:

Let me stand here till thou remember it.

JULIET:

I shall forget to have thee still stand there,
Remembering how I love thy company.

ROMEO:

And I'll still stay, to have thee still forget,
Forgetting any other home but this.

JULIET:

'Tis almost morning, I would have thee gone.
Good night, good night.
Parting is such sweet sorrow,
That I shall say good night, till it be morrow.

ROMEO:

Sleep dwell upon thine eyes, peace in thy breast.
Would I were sleep and peace, so sweet to rest.

NARRATOR:

Now Romeo hurries to the cell of Friar Laurence to tell
his kind old friend about his love and beg his help.

Two-shot of Friar and Romeo

FRIAR:

Be plain good son and homely in thy drift,
Riddling confession finds but riddling shrift.

ROMEO:

Then plainly know my heart's dear love is set
On the fair daughter of rich Capulet:
As mine on hers, so hers is set on mine,
And all combin'd, save what thou must combine
By holy marriage, and this I pray,
That thou consent to marry us to-day.

FRIAR:

Holy Saint Francis what a change is here?
But come young waverer, come go with me,
In one respect I'll thy assistant be:
For this alliance may so happy prove,
To turn your households' rancour to pure love.
Moving quickly off camera

ROMEO:

O let us hence, I stand on sudden haste.

FRIAR:

Wisely and slow, they stumble that run fast.

NARRATOR:

Morning comes and Juliet sends her old, devoted Nurse
to seek out Romeo and learn of his intent.
Two-shot of Nurse and Romeo

NURSE:

As I told you, my young Lady bid me inquire you out.

ROMEO:

Bid her devise
Some means to come to Shrift this afternoon,
And there she shall at Friar Laurence' cell
Be shriv'd and married: here is for thy pains.
Romeo offers purse to Nurse

NURSE:

No, truly, sir, not a penny.

ROMEO:

Go to, I say you shall.
Nurse takes purse

NURSE:

This afternoon, sir, well she shall be there.
Two-shot of Nurse and Juliet

JULIET:

O God she comes, O honey Nurse what news?

Now good sweet Nurse, O Lord, why look'st thou sad?
NURSE:

I am a-weary, give me leave a while,
Fie how my bones ache, what a jaunce have I had.
JULIET:

I would thou hadst my bones, and I thy news:
Nay come I pray thee to speak, good good Nurse speak.
NURSE:

Jesu, what haste, can you not stay a while?
Do you not see that I am out of breath?
JULIET:

How are thou out of breath, when thou hast breath
To say to me that thou art out of breath?
Is thy news good or bad? Answer to that.
What says he of our marriage, what of that?
NURSE:

Lord how my head aches, what a head have I!
It beats as it would fall in twenty pieces.
My back, o' t' other side, ah my back, my back!
JULIET:

Sweet, sweet, sweet Nurse, tell me what says my love?
NURSE:

Your love says like an honest gentleman, and a
courteous, and a kind, and a handsome, and I
warrant a virtuous . . . where is your mother?
JULIET:

Where is my mother, why she is within,
Where should she be? How oddly thou repliest:
Your love says like an honest gentleman,
Where is your mother?
NURSE:

Henceforward do your messages yourself.
JULIET:

Here's such a coil, come what says Romeo?
NURSE:
Have you got leave to go to shrift today?
JULIET:
I have.
NURSE:
Then hie you hence to Friar Laurence' cell,
There stays a husband to make you a wife!
NARRATOR:
So, at the Friar's cell they meet, and hear him say . . .
Three-shot of Friar, Romeo, and Juliet
FRIAR:
Come, come with me, and we will make short work.
For by your leaves, you shall not stay alone,
Till holy Church incorporate two in one.
Close on Narrator
NARRATOR:
Soon from the sunlit joy of noon the youthful lovers are
enshadowed. Tybalt, a Capulet and cousin to Juliet, in
a hot-tempered quarrel kills Mercutio, Romeo's friend.
Then, in revenge and provoked by Tybalt, Romeo kills
Tybalt and is doomed by the duke to immediate banish-
ment.
Two-shot of Nurse and Juliet
JULIET:
Banished, that one word banished,
Hath slain ten thousand Tybalts: Romeo is banished,
There is no end, no limit, measure bound,
In that word's death, no words can that woe sound.
NURSE: *(comforting Juliet)*
Hie to your chamber, I'll find Romeo
To comfort you.
Takes ring from her finger and gives it to Nurse.

JULIET:

O find him, give this ring to my true knight,
And bid him come, to take his last farewell.

Three-shot of Nurse, Friar, and Romeo

NURSE:

O holy Friar, O tell me holy Friar,
Where is my Lady's lord. Where's Romeo?

FRIAR:

There on the ground,
With his own tears made drunk.

ROMEO:

Oh tell me Friar, tell me,
In what vile part of this anatomy
Doth my name lodge?

He offers to stab himself, and the Nurse snatches the dagger away.

NURSE:

Ah?

FRIAR:

Hold thy desperate hand:
Art thou a man?
Thou hast amaz'd me. By my holy order,
I thought thy disposition better temper'd.
Hast thou slain Tybalt? Wilt thou slay thyself?
And slay thy Lady, that in thy life lives,
By doing damned hate upon thyself?
Take heed, take heed, for such die miserable.
Go get thee to thy love as was decreed,
Ascend her chamber, hence and comfort her.

Gives ring to Romeo

NURSE:

Here sir, a ring she bid me give you sir:
Hie you, make haste.

NARRATOR:

Romeo does make haste, and steals a farewell moment
with his Juliet before the break of day must send him to
his banishment. Meanwhile, her parents plot to marry
Juliet to the County Paris within the week.

Two-shot of Romeo and Juliet on balcony

JULIET:

Wilt thou be gone? It is not yet near day:
It was the nightingale, and not the lark
That pierc'd the fearful hollow of thine ear,
Nightly she sings on yon pomegranate tree,
Believe me love, it was the nightingale.

ROMEO:

It was the lark, the herald of the morn:
No nightingale: look love what envious streaks
Do lace the severing clouds in yonder East:
Night's candles are burnt out, and jocund day
Stands tiptoe on the misty mountain tops,
I must be gone and live, or stay and die.

JULIET:

Yond light is not daylight, I know it I:
Therefore stay yet, thou needs not to be gone.

Embracing Juliet

ROMEO:

I have more care to stay, than will to go:
Come death and welcome, Juliet wills it so.
How is't my soul? Let's talk, it is not day.

JULIET:

It is, it is, hie hence be gone away:
It is the lark that sings so out of tune,
Straining harsh discords, and unpleasing sharps.
So now be gone, more light and light it grows.

ROMEO:

More light and light, more dark and dark our woes.
Off camera
NURSE:
Your Lady mother is coming to your chamber,
The day is broke, be wary, look about.
JULIET:
Then window let day in, and let life out.
ROMEO:
Farewell, farewell, one kiss and I'll descend.
He kisses Juliet
JULIET:
O think'st thou we shall ever meet again?
ROMEO:
I doubt it not, and all these woes shall serve
For sweet discourses in our times to come.
JULIET:
O God, I have an ill-divining soul,
Methinks I see thee now, thou art so low,
As one dead in the bottom of a tomb,
Either my eyesight fails, or thou look'st pale.
ROMEO:
And trust me love, in my eye so do you:
Dry sorrow drinks our blood. Adieu, adieu.
Two-shot of Lady Capulet and Juliet
LADY CAPULET:
Ho daughter, are you up?
Why how now Juliet?
JULIET:
Madam I am not well.
LADY CAPULET:
Evermore weeping for your cousin's death?
What wilt thou wash him from his grave with tears?
But now I'll tell thee joyful tidings girl.

JULIET:

And joy comes well in such a needy time,

What are they, I beseech your Ladyship.

LADY CAPULET:

Well, well, thou hast a careful father, child,

One who to put thee from thy heaviness,

Hath sorted out a sudden day of joy,

That thou expect'st not, nor I look'd not for.

JULIET:

Madam in happy time, what day is that?

LADY CAPULET:

Marry my child, early next Thursday morn,

The gallant young, and noble gentleman,

The County Paris at Saint Peter's Church,

Shall happily make thee there a joyful bride.

JULIET:

Now by Saint Peter's Church, and Peter too,

He shall not make me there a joyful bride.

I pray you tell my Lord and Father, Madam,

I will not marry yet, and what I do, I swear

It shall be Romeo, whom you know I hate,

Rather than Paris, these are news indeed.

LADY CAPULET:

Here comes your father, tell him so yourself.

Capulet enters

CAPULET:

Have you deliver'd to her our decree?

LADY CAPULET:

Ay sir, but she will none, she gives you thanks.

CAPULET:

How, she will none? Doth she not count her blest,

Unworthy as she is, that we have wrought

So worthy a gentleman to be her bridegroom?

JULIET: *(She kneels down)*
Good father, I beseech you on my knees,
Hear me with patience, but to speak a word.
CAPULET:
Hang thee young baggage, disobedient wretch,
I tell thee what, get thee to church a' Thursday,
Or never after look me in the face.
Speak not, reply not, do not answer me.
Look to 't, think on 't, I do not use to jest.
Thursday is near, lay hand on heart, advise,
And you be mine, I'll give you to my friend,
And you be not, hang, beg, starve, die in the streets,
For by my soul I'll ne'er acknowledge thee:
Trust to 't, bethink you, I'll be forsworn.
JULIET:
Is there no pity sitting in the clouds
That sees into the bottom of my grief?
O sweet my Mother cast me not away,
Delay this marriage for a month, a week.
LADY CAPULET:
Talk not to me, for I'll not speak a word,
Do as thou wilt, for I have done with thee.
Capulet and Lady Capulet exit off camera. Nurse enters.
JULIET:
O God, O Nurse, how shall this be prevented?
NURSE:
I think it best you married with the County.
I think you are happy in this second match.
JULIET:
Speakest thou from thy heart?
NURSE:
And from my soul too.
Else beshrew them both.

JULIET:

Go in, and tell my Lady I am gone,
Having displeas'd my father, to Laurence' cell,
To make confession, and to be absolv'd.

NURSE:

Marry I will, and this is wisely done.
Nurse exits
Close on Juliet

JULIET:

I'll to the Friar to know his remedy,
If all else fail, myself have power to die.
Two-shot of Juliet and Friar

FRIAR:

Take thou this vial, and this distilled liquor drink.
And in this borrow'd likeness of shrunk death
Thou shalt continue two and forty hours,
And then awake as from a pleasant sleep.
Now when the Bridegroom in the morning comes,
To rouse thee from thy bed, there art thou dead:
Then as the manner of our country is,
In thy best robes uncovered on the bier,
Thou shalt be borne to that same ancient vault,
Where all the kindred of the Capulets lie;
In the meantime against thou shalt awake,
Shall Romeo by my letters know our drift,
And hither shall he come, and he and I
Will watch thy waking, and that very night
Shall Romeo bear thee hence to Mantua.
And this shall free thee from this present shame.

JULIET:

Give me, give me.
*Lady Capulet enters. Two-shot of Lady Capulet and
Juliet*

LADY CAPULET:

What are you busy ho? Need you my help?

JULIET:

No Madam.

LADY CAPULET:

Good night.

Get thee to bed and rest, for thou hast need.

After Lady Capulet exits close on Juliet. She drinks the potion, falls asleep. Dissolve.

JULIET:

Farewell, God knows when we shall meet again.

Romeo, I come, this do I drink to thee.

NARRATOR:

With Romeo now in banishment, Juliet takes the sleep-invoking potion, hoping that when she wakens from the trance the faithful friar will bring Romeo and her together that they may elope to Mantua. So, when the day breaks, the day she is to marry Paris, the nurse comes in to rouse her from her death-like sleep.

Nurse approaches the bed where Juliet lies. Upon discovering Juliet apparently dead, she screams. Lady Capulet and Capulet enter, to freeze in shocked horror.

NURSE:

Mistress, mistress Juliet, fast I warrant her she,

Why lamb, Lady, fie you slug-a-bed,

Why love I say, Madam, sweetheart,

My Lord, My Lady!

Close on Narrator

NARRATOR:

Romeo, hearing the news and believing his Juliet dead, secures poison from an apothecary and hurries to the Capulet tomb prepared to die beside his bride.

Juliet, appearing dead, is lying on a bier.

ROMEO:

O my Love, my wife,
Death that hath suck'd the honey of thy breath,
Hath had no power yet upon thy beauty:
Eyes look your last: Arms take your last embrace:
Thus with a kiss I die.
Romeo takes poison and falls dead.
Friar Lawrence enters tomb, finds Romeo dead.

FRIAR:

Romeo. Ah what an unkind hour
Is guilty of this lamentable chance!
The Lady stirs.
Juliet awakens

JULIET:

O comfortable Friar, where is my Lord?
I do remember well where I should be:
And here I am, where is my Romeo?

FRIAR:

Lady, come from that nest
Of death, contagion and unnatural sleep:
A greater power than we can contradict
Hath thwarted our intents, come come away,
Thy husband in the tomb with thee lies dead.
Stay not to question, for the watch is coming,
Come go good Juliet, I dare no longer stay.
Friar exits

JULIET:

Go get thee hence, for I will not away.
What's here? A cup clos'd in my true love's hand?
Poison I see hath been his timeless end.
Yea noise? Then I'll be brief. O happy dagger.
This is thy sheath, there rust and let me die.
Juliet stabs herself and falls across Romeo's body.

Close on narrator

NARRATOR:

Oh, house of Montague, and house of Capulet,
See what a scourge is laid upon your hate.
Go hence to have more talk of these sad things.
Some shall be pardoned, and some punished.
For never was a story of more woe,
Than this of Juliet and her Romeo.

Curtain

4
MACBETH

Macbeth

Synopsis

Witches, ghosts, murders, and villains are the stuff of melodrama, and *Macbeth* has them all. Right in the opening scene three weird hags tell us that something foul is afoot. They tell us again a little later when Macbeth stumbles on them and is amazed, if not too displeased, when they hail him not merely as the Thane of Glamis, which he is, but as the Thane of Cawdor, which would be a decided step up the political ladder. Then, as though that were not enough to pique the zeal of any ambitious aspirant, the witches hail him as "King hereafter."

King of Scotland! That is something to write home about. He does just that, and when Lady Macbeth reads his message her ambition is fired even more than that of her husband. She is not only ambitious, but ruthless, and worries lest her husband be too soft to take advantage of any occasion to advance himself.

On his way home, Macbeth learns that he is indeed Thane of Cawdor, that gentleman having been recently killed, and he learns also that Duncan, the present King of Scotland, is coming to the Macbeth castle to pay a social call.

"Duncan comes here tonight" he tells his excited wife, which is all she needs to start plotting. It would be simple enough to slit King Duncan's throat while he sleeps in the Macbeth house. Simple perhaps, but horrible, so horrible that Macbeth is reluctant to fall in with his wife's plan, but the lady goads, and Macbeth, proving that he is not the coward his wife calls him, does the horrible deed.

As is the case with crime, one awful sin begets another. If Macbeth is to secure the crown, one Banquo, a legitimate contender, must be put out of the way. Thugs do this job for Macbeth, but the deed is heavy on Macbeth's conscience and he sees the ghost of Banquo sitting at the head of a banquet the Macbeths are giving in celebration. Macbeth is so unnerved that he makes a spectacle of himself before the guests, but Lady Macbeth says her husband is not well and bids everyone leave at once. Alone with her husband, she chides him for being a weakling, suggesting that if he wants to be a king he should act like a king.

King he is by now, but uneasy is the head that wears the crown, and Macbeth goes again in search of the three weird hags, hoping their magic can conjure up some solution to his mounting problem. Instead, they counsel him to beware Macduff, a fellow Scot who is lining up forces against the murderous King Macbeth. Of course they do give him some assurance. "None of woman born will harm Macbeth," they chant, and add that Macduff will not come to Dunsinane, Macbeth's place of residence, until the forests of Birnam be moved to Dunsinane.

Since men are born of women and trees are not in the habit of uprooting themselves and marching to another location, the prophecy, we might think, should have satisfied Macbeth, but, being already so deep in blood he reasons that he may as well wade deeper, so orders the total destruction of the Macduff family, and

Lady Macduff and her innocent children are mercilessly murdered. Not Macduff, however! He is safe in England, raising an army to march against the bloodthirsty King Macbeth.

While Macbeth consorts with witches, Lady Macbeth walks in her sleep. Carrying a lighted taper, she walks downstairs and into the unseen presence of her maid and a doctor whom the suspicious maid has summoned to watch and wait for just such a moment. Not only does the distraught lady walk, but she talks, and what she says is as hair-raising as it is revealing! What she says is noted by the maid and the doctor, who jots down her words. " . . . who would have thought the old man to have had so much blood in him. . . . What, will these hands ne'er be clean? . . . Here's the smell of the blood still: all the perfumes of Arabia will not sweeten this little hand. . . . I tell you yet again Banquo's buried: he cannot come out on's grave." So sobs and mutters the guilty queen, and the next we hear of her is the news that she is dead by her own hand.

The bad news reaches Macbeth at a bad time. "She should have died hereafter," he says and turns to another piece of fearful news, which is that, the prophecy of the witches notwithstanding, Macduff, with a large company of armed men, is on his way to Dunsinane. More terrifying still is the sudden realization that the woods of Birnam are moving toward the Dunsinane castle. Macduff's soldiers have chopped down trees, which they are using as camouflage as they advance.

Suddenly, Macbeth is confronted by the man he most fears, Macduff. "Of all men else I have avoided thee," he says. Then, his faith in the prophecy of the witches unshaken, he declares that no man born of woman can harm him. Whereupon Macduff declares he was "from his mother's womb untimely ripp'd," so is no child of woman by ordinary birth.

With the battle raging around him Macbeth cries, "Lay on Macduff, and damn'd be him that first cries 'Hold, enough!'" They go out fighting, and a moment later Macduff reenters with the head of Macbeth.

So ends a bloody play of the bloody times of ancient Scotland—a tale of horror, but told in a misty mood of awe and pity.

Macbeth

(Stage directions are in italics)

First Witch	Lady Macbeth	Doctor
Second Witch	Murderer	Gentlewoman
Third Witch	Lennox	Officer
Narrator	Lady Macduff	Macduff
Macbeth	Messenger	

> *Note*: The Narrator may play several of the incidental roles, in which case the following should be inserted in the Narrator's first speech: "I am the Narrator in this short version of the play, but in the telling of the tale I am actor, too, so you will see me first as one character, then another."

Narrator enters and takes position at a podium down right

The Three Witches enter left, encircling the stage as they chant their lines

FIRST WITCH:

When shall we three meet again?

In thunder, lightning, or in rain?

SECOND WITCH:

When the hurly-burly's done,

When the battle's lost, and won.

THIRD WITCH:

That will be ere the set of sun.

105

ALL:

Fair is foul, and foul is fair,

Hover through the fog and filthy air.

Exeunt Witches up right

NARRATOR:

So opens William Shakespeare's tragedy of Macbeth, a bloody murder mystery out of the lore of ancient, misty Scotland. Now to the weird sisters three again, who hail the Scottish thane, Macbeth.

Sound of drum. The Witches enter up right, encircling the stage and ending in a picturization up right.

THIRD WITCH:

A drum, a drum: Macbeth doth come.

ALL:

The Weird Sisters, hand in hand,

Posters of the sea and land,

Thus do go, about, about.

Macbeth enters down left

MACBETH:

What are these?

Live you, or are you aught that man may question?

Speak if you can: what are you?

FIRST WITCH:

All hail Macbeth, hail to thee Thane of Glamis.

SECOND WITCH:

All hail Macbeth, hail to thee Thane of Cawdor.

THIRD WITCH:

All hail Macbeth, that shalt be King hereafter.

Witches run off right, laughing

MACBETH:

King hereafter!

NARRATOR:

As Macbeth exits slowly up right

Who are these weird creatures who prophesy that he,

Macbeth, will one day be a king? Duncan is king. Macbeth is only thane. Yet, while he ponders, word comes from the king that he is now made Thane of Cawdor, exactly as the witches had foretold. Marvel of marvels—he must send word of this unto his wife. *Lady Macbeth enters down left reading a letter.*

LADY MACBETH:

"They met me in the day of success: and I have learn'd by the perfect'st report, they have more in them than mortal knowledge. When I burnt in desire to question them further, they made themselves air, into which they vanish'd. Whiles I stood rapt in the wonder of it, came missives from the King, who all-hail'd me Thane of Cawdor, by the which title before, these Weird Sisters saluted me, and referr'd me to the coming on of time, with hail King that shalt be."

And shalt be

What thou art promis'd: yet do I fear thy nature,

It is too full o' th' milk of human kindness,

To catch the nearest way.

NARRATOR:

The lady may be right. Yet strangely, strangely, opportunity opens wide. Returning home, Macbeth is told King Duncan rides forth to visit in the castle of Macbeth. *Enter Macbeth up right, crossing to Lady Macbeth down left*

MACBETH:

My dearest love,

Duncan comes here to-night.

LADY MACBETH:

And when goes hence?

MACBETH:

To-morrow, as he purposes.

LADY MACBETH:

O never, Shall sun that morrow see.
He that's coming,
Must be provided for: and you shall put
This night's great business into my dispatch.

NARRATOR: *(as Lady Macbeth and Macbeth exeunt up
right)*

The king comes here tonight, and if he never leaves
this place alive, Macbeth would move one step further
to the throne. The thought is father to the wish.

MACBETH: *(entering up right)*

If it were done, when 'tis done, then 'twere well,
It were done quickly: if th' assassination
Could trammel up the consequence and catch
With his surcease, success: that but this blow
Might be the be-all, and the end-all. Here,
But here, upon this bank and school of time,
We'ld jump the life to come. But in these cases,
We still have judgment here.
He's here in double trust;
First, as I am his kinsman, and his subject,
Strong both against the deed: then, as his host,
Who should against his murtherer shut the door,
Not bear the knife myself. I have no spur
To prick the sides of my intent, but only
Vaulting Ambition, which o'erleaps itself,
And falls on th' other.

Lady Macbeth reenters up right. Macbeth crosses to her.

How now? What news?

LADY MACBETH:

He has almost supp'd: why have you left the chamber?

MACBETH:

Hath he ask'd for me?

LADY MACBETH:
Know you not, he has?

MACBETH:
We will proceed no further in this business.

LADY MACBETH:
Art thou afear'd
To be the same in thine own act, and valour,
As thou art in desire? Wouldst thou have that
Which thou esteem'st the ornament of life,
And live a coward in thine own esteem?
Letting I dare not, wait upon I would,
Like the poor cat i' th' adage.

MACBETH:
Prithee peace:
I dare do all that may become a man,
Who dares do more, is none.

LADY MACBETH:
What beast was't then
That made you break this enterprise to me?
When you durst do it, then you were a man.

MACBETH:
If we should fail?

LADY MACBETH:
We fail?
But screw your courage to the sticking-place,
And we'll not fail: when Duncan is asleep,
(Whereto the rather shall his hard day's journey
Soundly invite him)
What cannot you and I perform upon
Th' unguarded Duncan?

MACBETH:
Bring forth men-children only:
For thy undaunted mettle should compose

Nothing but males.

Away. . . .

Lady Macbeth exits right

. . . and mock the time with fairest show,
False face must hide what the false heart doth know.
Is this a dagger, which I see before me,
The handle toward my hand? Come, let me clutch thee:
I have thee not, and yet I see thee still.
Art thou not, fatal vision, sensible
To feeling, as to sight? or art thou but
A dagger of the mind,
I see thee yet, in form as palpable,
As this which now I draw.
Thou marshall'st me the way that I was going,
And such an instrument I was to use.

A bell rings.

I go, and it is done: the bell invites me.
Hear it not, Duncan, for it is a knell,
That summons thee to Heaven, or to Hell.

NARRATOR: *(as Macbeth exits up right)*
He moves, almost as in the spell of trance, knowing the
guards are in a drunken stupor, thanks to the ingenious
hospitality of his wife.

Enter Lady Macbeth up right

LADY MACBETH:
That which hath made them drunk, hath made me bold:
What hath quench'd them, hath given me fire.
Hark, peace: it was the owl that shriek'd,
He is about it, the doors are open.
Alack, I am afraid they have awak'd,
And 'tis not done: Had he not resembled
My father as he slept, I had done 't.

Macbeth enters right
My husband!
MACBETH:
I have done the deed:
Didst thou not hear a noise?
LADY MACBETH:
I heard the owl scream, and the crickets cry.
Did not you speak?
MACBETH:
When?
LADY MACBETH:
Now.
MACBETH:
As I descended?
LADY MACBETH:
Ay.
MACBETH:
Hark.
LADY MACBETH:
These deeds must not be thought
After these ways: so, it will make us mad.
MACBETH:
Methought I heard a cry, Sleep no more:
Macbeth does murther Sleep, the innocent Sleep,
Sleep that knits up the ravell'd sleeve of care,
The death of each day's life.
LADY MACBETH:
Go get some water,
And wash this filthy witness from your hand.
A knock is heard.
MACBETH:
Whence is that knocking?

How is't with me, when every noise appals me?
Will all great Neptune's Ocean wash this blood
Clean from my hand?

LADY MACBETH:

My hands are of your colour: but I shame
To wear a heart so white.

Knock

I hear a knocking at the south entry:
A little water clears us of this deed.
How easy is it then?

Knock

MACBETH:

Wake Duncan with thy knocking:
I would thou could'st.

NARRATOR: *(as Macbeth and Lady Macbeth exeunt up left)*

Duncan is dead. Macbeth has killed the king, and aided
by his wife, has put the blame on Duncan's sons who
now have fled the land. King of all Scotland now,
Macbeth is fearful of the rivals to his throne, especially
the Scottish lord named Banquo. Banquo is a threat.
Banquo must go. Yet Banquo is expected at the royal
feast tonight, but Banquo, it is said, is dead.

*Macbeth enters up left and crosses to meet the Murderer,
who enters down left.*

MACBETH:

There's blood upon thy face.

MURDERER:

'Tis Banquo's then.

MACBETH:

Is he dispatch'd?

MURDERER:

My Lord, his throat is cut.

MACBETH:

Thou art the best o' th' cut-throats.

Get thee gone.

Exit Murderer down left

NARRATOR:

Banquo is dead but, as the royal banquet proceeds, an unexpected guest appears, the ghost of Banquo. We are to imagine the presence of the other guests; the ghost of Banquo is seen only by Macbeth.

LADY MACBETH: *(entering up left and joining Macbeth, who has crossed to up right center.)*

My Royal Lord,

You do not give the cheer.

MACBETH:

Sweet remembrancer:

Now good digestion wait on appetite.

LADY MACBETH:

May't please your Highness sit.

MACBETH:

Here had we now our country's honour, roof'd,

Were the grac'd person of our Banquo present.

LADY MACBETH:

His absence, Sir,

Lays blame upon his promise. Please't your Highness

To grace us with your royal company?

MACBETH:

The table's full.

LADY MACBETH:

Here is a place reserv'd, Sir.

MACBETH:

Where?

LADY MACBETH:

Here, my good Lord.

What is't that moves your Highness?

MACBETH: *(seeing the ghost of Banquo)*

Which of you have done this?

LADY MACBETH:

What, my good Lord?

MACBETH:

Thou canst not say I did it: never shake

Thy gory locks at me.

LADY MACBETH: *(to guests)*

His Highness is not well. Sit, worthy friends:

My Lord is often thus.

(aside to Macbeth) Are you a man?

MACBETH:

If I stand here, I saw him.

This is more strange

Than such a murther is.

LADY MACBETH:

My worthy Lord

Your noble friends do lack you.

MACBETH:

I do forget:

Do not muse at me, my most worthy friends,

I have a strange infirmity, which is nothing

To those that know me. Come, love and health to all,

Then I'll sit down: give me some wine, fill full.

I drink to th' general joy o' th' whole table,

And to our dear friend Banquo, whom we miss:

Would he were here;

Sees the ghost again

Avaunt, and quit my sight, let the earth hide thee.

Hence horrible shadow,

Unreal mockery hence. *(laughs hysterically)*

As the ghost apparently vanishes . . .
Why so, being gone
I am a man again.
LADY MACBETH: *(to guests)*
I pray you speak not: he grows worse and worse:
Question enrages him: at once, good night.
Stand not upon the order of your going,
But go at once. A kind good night to all.
NARRATOR: *(as Lady Macbeth exits down left and Macbeth stands in a daze)*
The banquet abruptly breaks up. The guests depart, but Banquo's ghost still haunts the guilty conscience of Macbeth.
MACBETH:
I will to-morrow
(And betimes I will) to the Weird Sisters.
More shall they speak: for now I am bent to know
By the worst means, the worst; for mine own good,
All causes shall give way. I am in blood
Stepp'd in so far, that should I wade no more,
Returning were as tedious as go o'er.
NARRATOR: *(as Macbeth exits up left)*
To the misty moor he goes again, to the Wierd Sisters and their prophecies.
The Three Witches enter up right, circling stage and forming a picturization up right.
FIRST WITCH:
Round about the cauldron go:
In the poison'd entrails throw.
ALL:
Double, double, toil and trouble;
Fire burn, and cauldron bubble.

SECOND WITCH:

By the pricking of my thumbs,
Something wicked this way comes:
Open locks, whoever knocks.

Enter Macbeth up left

MACBETH:

How now you secret, black, and midnight hags:
What is't you do?

ALL:

A deed without a name.

MACBETH:

I conjure you, by that which you profess,
(Howe'er you come to know it) answer me
To what I ask you.

FIRST WITCH:

Macbeth, Macbeth, Macbeth:
Beware Macduff,
Beware the Thane of Fife.

SECOND WITCH:

Macbeth, Macbeth, Macbeth.

MACBETH:

Had I three ears, I'ld hear thee.

SECOND WITCH:

Be bloody, bold, and resolute:
Laugh to scorn
The power of man: for none of woman born
Shall harm Macbeth.

MACBETH:

Then live Macduff: what need I fear of thee?

THIRD WITCH:

Macbeth shall never vanquish'd be, until
Great Birnam Wood, to high Dunsinane Hill
Shall come against him.

Witches exeunt up right

MACBETH:

That will never be.

Enter Lennox down left

I did hear the galloping of horse.

Who was't came by?

LENNOX:

'Tis two or three my Lord, that bring you word:

Macduff is fled to England.

MACBETH:

Fled to England?

LENNOX:

Ay, my good Lord.

Lennox exits down left

MACBETH:

Time, thou anticipat'st my dread exploits:

The castle of Macduff, I will surprise,

Seize upon Fife: give to th' edge o' th' sword

His wife, his babes, and all unfortunate souls

That trace him in his line. No boasting like a fool,

This deed I'll do, before this purpose cool!

NARRATOR: *as Macbeth exits up right*

Beware Macduff. Beware Macduff, though he be fled to
England leaving behind his bewildered wife and helpless
children.

LADY MACDUFF: *entering up left*

What had he done, to make him fly the land?

His flight was madness: when our actions do not,

Our fears do make us traitors.

To leave his wife, to leave his babes,

His mansion, and his titles, in a place

From whence himself does fly? He loves us not,

He wants the natural touch.

Enter messenger right

MESSENGER:

Bless you fair Dame.

I doubt some danger does approach you nearly.

If you will take a homely man's advice,

Be not found here: hence with your little ones.

Heaven preserve you, I dare abide no longer.

Exit messenger

LADY MACDUFF: *(sitting on bench down left)*

Whither should I fly?

I have done no harm. But I remember now

I am in this earthly world: where to do harm

Is often laudable, to do good sometime

Accounted dangerous folly. Why then, alas,

Do I put up that womanly defence,

To say I have done no harm?

She exits down left

NARRATOR:

They come, the murderous henchmen of Macbeth, and
slay her brutally and slay her children. Maddened by
guilt and fear, Macbeth will slaughter aimlessly, not
knowing that Macduff, hearing of the saddening and
sickening crime, will return with Banquo's son to Scotland determined to wreak vengeance upon the villainous
king. Meanwhile, the queen, walking the castle in her
sleep, babbles insanely of her bloody guilt.

Doctor and Gentlewoman enter down left

DOCTOR:

I have two nights watch'd with you, but can perceive no
truth in your report. When was it she last walked? *(Sitting on bench down left)*

GENTLEWOMAN:

Since his Majesty went into the field, I have seen her

rise from her bed, throw her nightgown upon her, unlock her closet, take forth paper, fold it, write upon 't, read it, afterwards seal it, and again return to bed; yet all this while in a most fast sleep.

Lady Macbeth enters up left and crosses to up right

Lo you, here she comes: and upon my life fast asleep: observe her, stand close.

DOCTOR:

You see her eyes are open.

GENTLEWOMAN:

Ay, but their sense is shut.

DOCTOR:

What is it she does now?
Look how she rubs her hands.

GENTLEWOMAN:

It is an accustom'd action with her, to seem thus washing her hands.

LADY MACBETH:

Yet here's a spot.

DOCTOR:

Hark, she speaks.

LADY MACBETH:

Out damned spot: out I say. One: two: why then 'tis time to do 't: Hell is murky. Fie, my Lord, fie, a soldier, and afear'd? what need we fear? who knows it, when none can call our power to account: yet who would have thought the old man to have had so much blood in him. The Thane of Fife, had a wife: where is she now? What will these hands ne'er be clean? No more o' that, my Lord, no more o' that: you mar all with this starting. Here's the smell of the blood still: all the perfumes of Arabia will not sweeten this little hand. Oh, oh, oh. Wash your hands, put on your nightgown, look not so pale: I tell you yet again Banquo's buried: he cannot come out on's grave.

DOCTOR:

Even so?

LADY MACBETH:

To bed, to bed: there's knocking at the gate: come, come, come, come, give me your hand: what's done, cannot be undone. To bed, to bed, to bed.

Exit Lady Macbeth up left

DOCTOR:

Will she go now to bed?

GENTLEWOMAN:

Directly.

DOCTOR:

Foul whisperings are abroad: unnatural deeds
Do breed unnatural troubles.
More needs she the divine, than the physician:
God, God forgive us all. Look after her,
So good night,
My mind she has mated, and amaz'd my sight.
I think, but dare not speak.

GENTLEWOMAN:

Good night, good doctor.

Gentlewoman exits up left, Doctor down left

NARRATOR:

Now, while his guilt-stricken queen relives their awful deeds in dream, Macbeth prepares for battle, having heard that Macduff with armies will encounter him at Dunsinane.

Macbeth enters up right. Officer enters down left. Sound of women wailing off left is heard.

MACBETH:
What is that noise?

OFFICER:
It is the cry of women, my good Lord.

MACBETH:
Wherefore was that cry?

OFFICER:
The Queen, my Lord, is dead.
Macbeth holds, stunned, then waves the officer off. Officer exits down left.

MACBETH: *(crossing slowly to bench down left)*
She should have died hereafter:
There would have been a time for such a word:
To-morrow, and to-morrow, and to-morrow,
Creeps in this petty pace from day to day,
To the last syllable of recorded time:
And all our yesterdays, have lighted fools
The way to dusty death. Out, out, brief candle,
Life's but a walking shadow, a poor player,
That struts and frets his hour upon the stage,
And then is heard no more. *(rising, crossing
to up right center)* It is a tale
Told by an idiot, full of sound and fury
Signifying nothing.
Re-enter Officer
Thou comest to use thy tongue: thy story quickly.

OFFICER:
Gracious my Lord,
I should report that which I say I saw,
But know not how to do it.

MACBETH:
Well, say sir.

OFFICER:
As I did stand my watch upon the hill,

I look'd toward Birnam, and anon methought
The Wood began to move.

MACBETH:

Liar, and slave.
Fear not, Till Birnam Wood
Do come to Dunsinane; and now a wood
Comes toward Dunsinane!

Officer exits down left

NARRATOR:

The hills are now alive with soldiers of Macduff shielded
behind branches that look like trees moving toward the
terrified Macbeth. And now he is confronted by the mortal he most fears, the vengeful, brave Macduff.

Macduff enters up left

MACBETH:

Of all men else I have avoided thee:
But get thee back, my soul is too much charg'd
With blood of thine already.

MACDUFF: *(drawing his sword)*

I have no words,
My voice is in my sword, thou bloodier villain
Than terms can give thee out.

MACBETH:

Let fall thy blade on vulnerable crests,
I bear a charmed life, which must not yield
To one of woman born.

MACDUFF:

Despair thy charm,
And let the Angel whom thou still hast serv'd
Tell thee, Macduff was from his mother's womb
Untimely ripp'd.

MACBETH:

Accursed be that tongue that tells me so;

I will not yield
Though Birnam Wood be come to Dunsinane,
And thou oppos'd, being of no woman born,
Yet I will try the last.
Macbeth draws his sword, and they move off up right,
fighting.
Lay on Macduff
And damn'd be him, that first cries hold, enough.
NARRATOR: *(after Macbeth and Macduff exeunt)*
The fight was fierce. The finish swift. Here was no time
to first cry, "Hold, enough." Macduff cut off the head
of King Macbeth. So out, out, brief candle, as down to
dusty death our villain hero goes, a poor player, who
strutted his hour in sound and fury, and now is heard no
more.

Curtain

5
The Tragedy of
HAMLET

Hamlet

Synopsis

Stripped of its subplot, the story of *Hamlet* is simple. A young man called home from college at the death of his father is heartsick to discover that his mother has suddenly married his uncle, whom he suspects of having murdered his father. That terse, but arresting, statement is the thread from which the greatest of Shakespeare's plays is woven.

Hamlet, the young man, is a prince and the rightful heir to the throne of Denmark. The time is usually thought to be in the late Middle Ages. The place is Elsinore, in and around the castle.

Being a sensitive young man, Hamlet is distraught and depressed to find his mother, whom he adores, so soon married again, and to, of all people, his uncle, whom he does not like. Furthermore Uncle Claudius has neatly ensconced himself on the throne, which should rightfully have gone to Hamlet. There is wanton merriment in a house that should be steeped in mourning for the dead king, and that too rankles.

Friends, one in particular, his very dear friend Horatio, bring hair-raising news. Out on the parapet where the guard keeps watch, in the haunting mist, a "thing" has appeared three nights, and the friends swear it is the ghost of King Hamlet. Fearfully impressed, the Prince goes to see for himself, and the vision appears again. This time it talks to young Hamlet, declaring itself to

127

be the ghost of Hamlet's father and describing in detail how he was put to death by his brother, by the ingenious device of pouring poison in his ear while he slept.

Hamlet must now seek objective proof of the ghost's word, for he has sworn to avenge his father's murder.

Meanwhile there is an affair of the heart to work out. The Prince is involved with a sweet, wistful girl named Ophelia, daughter of the Prime Minister, Polonius. His concern for Ophelia, added to his anxiety over establishing the guilt of his uncle, provokes a conduct that worries his mother, and she wonders if her son, for whom she has a genuine fondness, is mentally off balance, an idea that her husband, the new king Claudius, is only too happy to promote, abetted by his ever-eager-to-please Prime Minister, Polonius. In an effort to prove Hamlet's madness they set a trap for him. Polonius persuades his daughter to wait for Hamlet while he and the King observe the encounter from behind a drapery.

In an honest, though painful, effort to break off his romance with Ophelia, Hamlet now tells her he never loved her, then declares he never gave her the memento she tries to return to him. Fighting his emotions and losing control, he chides Ophelia shamefully, then, suddenly aware that he is being spied upon by Polonius and his Uncle Claudius, he turns on her, asking where her father is. When she lies, saying he is at home, Hamlet flies into a rage, advising Ophelia to forget him and go into a nunnery, then storms off, leaving Ophelia bewildered and brokenhearted.

This is enough to convince Polonius and Claudius that Hamlet is mad, but we soon see that he has his wits about him as he plots with an old actor friend to insert special lines and business into a play to be performed later that evening for the King and all the Court.

In the play that the actors perform, the inserted scene devised by Hamlet depicts a king asleep and a suspicious-looking character stealthily pouring poison in the king's ear. Observing this, King Claudius leaps to his feet, calling for lights and putting a stop to the performance. Whereupon Hamlet clutches the arm of his friend, crying "Oh, good Horatio, I'll take the ghost's word . . . . Didst perceive?"

A moment later we see Claudius in the secrecy of his chamber trying to pray as he admits his horrible guilt. Hamlet appears and is about to run his sword through the kneeling King when he thinks better of it. To kill his uncle now, while he is at prayer, would send his soul to heaven, he reasons. Better to catch him in an act of licentiousness. Then, remembering that Polonius has told him his mother wants to see him in her chamber, he goes to join her.

Frightened by Hamlet's drawn sword, Gertrude, his mother, cries for help. Polonius, who is concealed behind the arras, where by previous arrangement with the Queen he is spying on Hamlet, then cries out. Hamlet, thinking Polonius is the King, thrusts his sword through the arras and kills the conniving old man. Then follows a terrifying scene with his mother, in which he accuses her of abetting Claudius in the murder of his father, then begs her not to love his uncle. He leaves, sorrowfully taking the body of Polonius away with him.

Gertrude tells Claudius immediately of her son's rash murdering of Polonius and the king orders his arrest and banishes him to England, where he is to be put to death.

Under the emotional strain of Hamlet's rejection of her and the news that Hamlet has killed her father, Ophelia goes quite mad. At this moment, Laertes, Ophelia's brother, returns to Elsinore under the impression that it was Claudius who has killed his father. When he is convinced by Claudius that it was Hamlet who killed Polonius, he is ready to fall in with a plot that Claudius devises for doing away with Hamlet who, it is learned, did not reach England but has returned to Denmark. Hamlet will be invited to fence with Laertes "purely for sport" for the entertainment of the King and Court. Laertes will arm himself with a foil, the tip of which is anointed with a fatal poison. The King will prepare a poisonous drink for Hamlet for double assurance.

Gertrude brings the sad news that the mad Ophelia has drowned herself in the river. Hamlet and Horatio pass through the graveyard on their way to the castle and there Hamlet discovers that the funeral procession is Ophelia's. Leaping into her grave, he defends his love for Ophelia and attacks Laertes. The King promptly parts them and later sends for Hamlet to fence with Laertes.

In the bout, Hamlet is wounded. Though the wound is slight, a mere scratch by the poisoned blade is fatal. Gertrude, not knowing it contains poison, takes the goblet the King has prepared and hands it to Hamlet to refresh him. "I'll play this bout first; set it by awhile," says Hamlet, so Gertrude lifts the goblet to her lips and drinks to Hamlet's success, unmindful of her husband's admonition not to drink it. She swoons and soon lies dying as the fencing continues, this time so furiously that each man disarms the other. In the scramble to regain their foils they unwittingly exchange swords. Now

Hamlet wounds Laertes, who, suddenly aware that he has been wounded by his own poisoned sword, confesses the plot to Hamlet and begs his forgiveness. Now it is discovered that the Queen is dead. Hamlet is stunned over the death of his mother. Then Laertes cries out that the King is to blame for the whole horrible business, reminding Hamlet that the sword he holds is the one tipped with poison. Thereupon Hamlet plunges his sword into the King, killing him instantly. Laertes, too, dies and Hamlet, weakening, falls into the arms of Horatio and makes his farewell, concluding with "The rest is silence."

"Good night, sweet Prince," says Horatio, as he tenderly holds his dying friend. "Good night, sweet Prince, and flights of angels sing thee to thy rest."

Hamlet

(Video directions are in italics)

CAST

Hamlet	Laertes
Narrator	Ophelia
Queen Gertrude	Ghost
King Claudius	Player
Horatio	Grave Digger
Polonius	Osric

Note: The Narrator may play several of the incidental roles, in which case the following should be inserted in the Narrator's first speech: "I am the Narrator in this short version of the play, but in the telling of the tale I am actor, too, so you will see me first as one character, then another."

Camera close on Hamlet

HAMLET:

To be or not to be—that is the question.

During the following narration dissolve to a long shot showing two thrones backed by a regal tapestry. In a moment, King Claudius and Queen Gertrude enter up stage. They smile and bow as though acknowledging applause. Then Claudius assists Gertrude to the throne and sits beside her, holding her hand and smiling at her.

NARRATOR: *(off camera)*

The tragedy of *Hamlet* by William Shakespeare is many things to many people, but in this vignette version it is a straight and simple story of a sensitive youth who,

132

finding that his world is out of joint, is loath yet spurred to put it right.

Hamlet enters and after a perfunctory bow to the Queen crosses to the opposite side where he remains standing aloof.

NARRATOR:

Put yourself in Hamlet's place: you are suddenly called home from college to attend your father's funeral. Added to this shock is the bewildering discovery that your mother, whom you adore, is married to your uncle, who now occupies the throne which you, as prince, should have inherited.

As Queen crosses to Hamlet dolly to two-shot of Gertrude and Hamlet.

NARRATOR:

It is small comfort to hear your mother say:

GERTRUDE:

Good Hamlet cast thy nighted color off, and let thine eye look like a friend on Denmark. Do not for ever with thy veiled lids seek for thy noble father in the dust.

Camera widens to three-shot to include Claudius as he enters to speak to Hamlet.

NARRATOR:

And it is less comforting still to hear the new King, your uncle, say:

CLAUDIUS:

'Tis sweet and commendable in your nature, Hamlet, to give these mourning duties to your father, but you must know your father lost a father, that father lost, lost his. We pray you throw to earth this unprevailing woe, and think of us as of a father.

As Hamlet turns away, Claudius and Gertrude exeunt, then camera comes close on Hamlet.

HAMLET:

That it should come to this, but two months dead, nay not so much, not two, so excellent a king, that was to this hyperion to a satyr, so loving to my mother that he might not beteem the winds of heaven visit her face too roughly. Heaven and earth, must I remember? Let me not think on 't; frailty, thy name is woman—married with my uncle, my father's brother, but no more like my father than I to Hercules. It is not, nor it cannot come to good. But break my heart, for I must hold my tongue.

Camera widens to include Horatio, who enters.

HORATIO:

Hail to your lordship!

HAMLET:

Horatio—or I do forget myself. And what make you from Wittenberg, Horatio? What is your affair in Elsinore?

HORATIO:

My lord, I came to see your father's funeral.

HAMLET:

I prithee do not mock me, fellow student. I think it was to see my mother's wedding.

HORATIO:

Indeed, my lord, it followed hard upon.

HAMLET:

My father—methinks I see my father.

HORATIO:

Where, my lord?

HAMLET:

In my mind's eye, Horatio.

HORATIO:

My lord, I think I saw him yesternight.

HAMLET:

Saw? Who?

HORATIO:

My lord, the king your father.

HAMLET:

The king my father?

HORATIO:

A figure like your father.

HAMLET:

Did you not speak to it?

HORATIO:

My lord, I did, but answer made it none.

HAMLET:

I will watch to-night. Perchance 'twill walk again.

Dissolve to three-shot of Polonius, Laertes, and Ophelia.
Polonius is engaged in pantomimic conversation and is
obviously giving Laertes advice.

NARRATOR: *(during the above shot)*

High in the court of King Claudius is Polonius, father
of Laertes and Ophelia, who is in love with Hamlet.
Laertes is off to France and Polonius has a word of
parting advice:

POLONIUS:

This above all, to thine own self be true, and it must
follow as the night the day thou canst not then be false
to any man. Farewell, my blessings season this in thee!

LAERTES:

Most humbly do I take my leave, my lord. Farewell,
Ophelia, and remember well what I have said to you.

OPHELIA:

'Tis in my memory locked, and you yourself shall keep
the key of it.

LAERTES:

Farewell.

Two-shot of Polonius and Ophelia as Laertes exits

POLONIUS:

How now, Ophelia, what is't he hath said to you?

OPHELIA:

So please you, something touching the Lord Hamlet.

POLONIUS:

What is between you? Give me up the truth.

OPHELIA:

He hath, my lord, of late made many tenders of his affection to me. And hath given countenance to his speech, my lord, with almost all the holy vows of heaven.

POLONIUS:

Do not believe his vows. I would not, in plain terms, from this time forth have you so slander any moment leisure as to give words or talk with the Lord Hamlet. *Camera close on Ophelia as she reacts with disappointment. Dissolve to two-shot of Hamlet and Horatio.*

NARRATOR:

Now you, as Hamlet, watch at the midnight hour with your friend, Horatio, for the vision of your father which he says he saw.

HORATIO:

Look my lord, it comes.

HAMLET:

Thou comest in such a questionable shape that I will speak to thee: I'll call thee Hamlet, King, father, royal Dane: O, answer me! *Camera close on Hamlet as voice of Ghost is heard off camera and on echo chamber*

GHOST:

I am thy father's spirit. If thou didst ever thy dear father love—

HAMLET:

O God!

GHOST:

—revenge his foul and most unnatural murder.

HAMLET:

Murder?

GHOST:

Murder most foul. Now, Hamlet, hear. 'Tis given out that, sleeping in my orchard, a serpent stung me. But know, thou noble youth, the serpent that did sting thy father's life now wears his crown.

HAMLET:

O my prophetic soul! My uncle?

GHOST:

Ay. Sleeping within my orchard, my custom always of the afternoon, thy uncle stole with the juice of cursed hebonon in a vial, and in the porches of my ears did pour the leperous distilment. The glowworm shows the matin to be near. Adieu, adieu, adieu. Remember me.

HAMLET:

Remember thee? Yes, by heaven!

During the following narration slow dissolve on Hamlet to two-shot of Polonius and Ophelia, who runs on in a state of agitation.

NARRATOR:

Your father murdered, and by your uncle. No wonder you behave most strangely when next you meet Ophelia, provoking her to pitiable bewilderment.

OPHELIA:

O my lord, my lord, I have been so affrighted!

POLONIUS:

With what, i' th' name of God?

OPHELIA:

My Lord Hamlet.

POLONIUS:

What, have you given him any hard words of late?

OPHELIA:

No, my good Lord; but as you did command I did repel his letters and denied his access to me.

POLONIUS:

That hath made him mad. Come, go we to the King. This must be known.

Exit Polonius. Camera holds on Ophelia, dissolving slowly to a medium shot of Claudius and Gertrude with their backs to the camera, watching Hamlet, who crosses upstage of them, unaware of their presence. As Hamlet exits, Gertrude and Claudius give each other a knowing look.

NARRATOR:

Brooding on madness begets a strange behavior and Claudius and Gertrude are ready to share the suspicion of madness now voiced by Polonius.

Medium shot of Claudius and Gertrude as Polonius enters excitedly with a letter.

POLONIUS:

My lord, my lord, I do think that I have found the very cause of Hamlet's lunacy.

CLAUDIUS:

O, speak of that! That do I long to hear.

GERTRUDE:

I doubt it is no other but the main, his father's death and our o'erhasty marriage.

POLONIUS:

My liege and madam, I have a daughter (have while she is mine) who in her duty and obedience, mark, hath given me this.

"O dear Ophelia, but that I love thee best, O most best, believe it. Adieu. Thine evermore, Hamlet."

CLAUDIUS:

Do you think 'tis this?

GERTRUDE:

It may be, very like.

During the following narration Gertrude, Claudius, and Polonius exchange significant glances. Dissolve to long shot of Hamlet and Player entering up stage and moving down toward camera as they pantomime conversation.

NARRATOR:

The ghost has spoken to you, Hamlet. You cannot forget. But if you are to avenge the death of your father you must have grounds more relative than this.

Two-shot of Hamlet and the Player

HAMLET:

Dost thou hear me, old friend? Cans't thou play "The Murder of Gonzago"?

PLAYER:

Ay, my lord.

HAMLET:

We'll ha't to-morrow night. You could for a need study a speech of some dozen or sixteen lines which I would set down and insert in't, could you not?

PLAYER:

Ay, my lord.

Player exits and Horatio enters as Hamlet summons him.

HAMLET:

Horatio?

HORATIO:

Here, sweet lord, at your service.

HAMLET:

I have heard that guilty creatures sitting at a play have

by the very cunning of the scene been struck so to the soul that presently they have proclaimed their malefactions. For murther, though it have no tongue, will speak with most miraculous organ. I'll have these players play something like the murther of my father before mine uncle. The play's the thing wherein I'll catch the conscience of the King.

During the following narration Hamlet starts to leave but stops as he sees Ophelia enter with a parcel of souvenirs, which she regards with sentiment. Ophelia is not aware of Hamlet and Horatio. Horatio, sizing up the situation, exits.

NARRATOR:

And if you catch the conscience of the King and know your uncle to be guilty, the awful thing you then must do must not be hindered, not even by Ophelia's love for you, or yours for her.

Two-shot of Hamlet and Ophelia as Ophelia becomes aware of Hamlet's presence

OPHELIA:

My lord, I have remembrances of yours that I have longed long to redeliver. I pray you, now receive them.

HAMLET:

No, not I, I never gave you aught.

OPHELIA:

My honored lord, you know right well you did, and with them words of so sweet breath composed as made the things more rich. Their perfume gone, take these again, for to the noble mind rich gifts wax poor when givers prove unkind. There, my lord.

HAMLET:

Are you honest?

OPHELIA:

My lord?

HAMLET:

Are you fair?

OPHELIA:

What means your lordship?

HAMLET:

I did love you once.

OPHELIA:

Indeed, my lord, you made me believe so.

HAMLET:

You should not have believed me.

Dolly back to medium shot of Hamlet and Ophelia.

I loved you not.

OPHELIA:

I was the more deceived.

HAMLET:

Get thee to a nunnery. Why wouldst thou be a breeder
of sinners? I am myself indifferent honest. We are arrant
knaves all; believe none of us. Go thy ways to a nunnery.

OPHELIA:

O, help him, you sweet heavens!

HAMLET:

If thou dost marry, I'll give thee this plague for thy
dowry: be thou as chaste as ice, as pure as snow, thou
shalt not escape calumny. Get thee to a nunnery. Go,
farewell. Or if thou wilt needs marry, marry a fool,
for wise men know well enough what monsters you make
of them. To a nunnery, go, and quickly, too.

OPHELIA:

O heavenly powers, restore him!

HAMLET:

I say we will have no more marriages. Those that are
married already—all but one—shall live. The rest shall

keep as they are. To a nunnery, go.

As Hamlet exits, camera comes close on Ophelia.

OPHELIA:

O, what a noble mind is here o'erthrown!

Camera holds on Ophelia, who continues to sob.

NARRATOR:

So you leave Ophelia heartbroken and bewildered.

Dissolve to long shot of Hamlet, pacing and carrying a dagger.

NARRATOR:

Now you are alone. What a rogue and peasant slave you are. With thoughts like these you ponder.

Camera close on Hamlet

HAMLET:

To be, or not to be—that is the question. Whether 'tis nobler in the mind to suffer the slings and arrows of outrageous fortune or to take arms against a sea of troubles and by opposing, end them. To die, to sleep— no more—and by that sleep of death to say we end the heartache, and the thousand natural shocks that flesh is heir to. 'Tis a consummation devoutly to be wished. To die, to sleep—to sleep—perchance to dream: ay, there's the rub, for in that sleep of death what dreams may come when we have shuffled off this mortal coil, must give us pause. There's the respect that makes calamity of so long life. For who would bear the whips and scorns of time, th' oppressor's wrong, the proud man's contumely, the pangs of despised love, the law's delay, the insolence of office, and the spurns that patient merit of th' unworthy takes, when he himself might his quietus make with a bare bodkin? Who would fardels bear, to grunt and sweat under a weary life, but that the dread of something after death, the undiscovered country from whose bourn no traveller returns, puzzles the will, and makes us rather bear those ills we have than fly to others that we know not of? Thus conscience does make cowards of us all.

Camera dollies back for long shot of Hamlet as he throws away the dagger.

As Narrator speaks, Hamlet stands for a moment, lost in thought, then with sudden decision hurries off.

NARRATOR:

That crisis passed, you hurry to instruct the players, now in a lighter mood.

Camera close on player as Hamlet speaks off camera

HAMLET:

Speak the speech, I pray you, as I pronounced it to you, trippingly on the tongue. For if you mouth it, as many of our players do, I had as lief the town crier spoke my lines.

Widen shot to include Hamlet as he moves in to ruffle the Player's hair good naturedly.

O, it offends me to the soul to hear a robustious peri-wigpated fellow tear a passion to tatters, to very rags. Suit the action to the word, the word to the action.

As voices are heard off camera:

I must be idle. They are coming to the play. Go make you ready.

As Narrator speaks, Hamlet and the Player exeunt in opposite directions and the shot dissolves to a two-shot of Claudius and Gertrude seated as though watching a play.

NARRATOR:

The play's the thing. And now, as Hamlet, you watch

for that tell-tale moment in the action and then . . .
Camera holds on Gertrude and Claudius as Hamlet speaks off camera.

HAMLET:

'e poisons him i' the garden for his estate. His name's Gonzago. You shall see anon how the murderer gets the love of Gonzago's wife.

Claudius rises in horror as Gertrude regards him.

GERTRUDE:

How fares my lord?

KING:

Give me some light. Away!

Claudius exits in panic followed by Gertrude. Dissolve to medium shot of Hamlet and Horatio, with Polonius entering immediately.

HAMLET:

Oh, good Horatio, I'll take the ghost's word for a thousand pound. Didst perceive?

HORATIO:

Very well, my lord.

POLONIUS:

My lord, the queen would speak with you, and presently.

HAMLET:

Do you see yonder cloud that's almost in shape of a camel?

POLONIUS:

By th' mass and 'tis, like a camel indeed.

HAMLET:

Methinks it is like a weasel.

POLONIUS:

It is backed like a weasel.

HAMLET:

Or like a whale.

POLONIUS:

Very like a whale.

HAMLET:

Then I will come to my mother by and by.

Long shot of Claudius praying

NARRATOR:

The king has flinched. His conscience has been pricked, and now you know your course. But on your way to see your mother as she bade you, you chance to find your uncle praying and disarmed.

CLAUDIUS:

Forgive me my foul murder.

Hamlet enters and, unseen by the praying Claudius, unsheathes his sword.

HAMLET:

Now might I do it pat, now he is a-praying, and now I'll do't. And so he goes to heaven, and so am I revenged? That would be scann'd. A villain kills my father, and for that I, his sole son, do this same villain send to heaven. No. Up, sword, and know thou a more horrid hent.

During the following narration Hamlet exits slowly. Camera holds on Claudius, who continues to pray, then dissolves to shot of Gertrude and Polonius as Polonius is hiding behind an arras of drapes.

NARRATOR:

So you procrastinate, put off the awful deed, yet knowing it must be done, but knowing not that at that very moment Polonius is hiding in your mother's room, hoping to spy on you. Now when you enter, murder is in your eyes, terrifying your mother.

Camera close on Gertrude, who is terrified

GERTRUDE:

What wilt thou do? Thou wilt not murther me?
Help, ho!

POLONIUS:

What, ho!

GERTRUDE:

Help!

*Camera dollies back to include Hamlet standing by
drawn drapes*

NARRATOR:

Hearing a cry behind the drawn drapes and thinking
it is the king, your uncle, you thrust.

HAMLET:

Dead for a ducat, dead!

GERTRUDE:

O me, what hast thou done?

HAMLET:

Nay, I know not. Is it the King?

GERTRUDE:

O, what a rash and bloody deed is this!

HAMLET:

A bloody deed—almost as bad, good Mother, as kill
a king, and marry with his brother.

GERTRUDE:

As kill a king?

HAMLET:

Ay, lady, it was my word.

*Hamlet pulls aside the drapes and is horrified at what he
sees. He kneels to examine the body he has stabbed.*

Thou wretched, rash, intruding fool, farewell!
I took thee for thy better.

*In utter anxiety Gertrude paces and wrings her hands.
Hamlet rises to address her.*

Leave wringing of your hands. Peace, sit you down.

And let me wring your heart. Look here upon this picture . . .

Hamlet compares a miniature he is wearing about his neck with one Gertrude is wearing about her neck.

. . . and upon this, the counterfeit presentment of two brothers. This was your husband. Here *is* your husband, like a mildewed ear blasting his wholesome brother. Have you eyes? Could you on this fair mountain leave to feed and batten on this moor? Ha! Have you eyes? You cannot call it love, for at your age the heyday in the blood is tame, it's humble, and waits upon the judgment, and what judgment would step from this to this?

GERTRUDE:

O Hamlet, speak no more. Thou turn'st mine eyes into my very soul, and there I see such black and grained spots as will not leave their tinct.

HAMLET:

Nay, but to live in the rank sweat of an enseamed bed, stewed in corruption, honeying and making love over the nasty sty—

GERTRUDE:

O, speak to me no more. These words like daggers enter in mine ears.

HAMLET:

A murtherer and a villain, a slave that is not twentieth part the tithe of your precedent lord . . .

GERTRUDE:

Speak no more!

HAMLET:

. . . a vice of kings, a cutpurse of the empire and the rule . . .

GERTRUDE:

No more!

HAMLET:

. . . that from a shelf the precious diadem stole and put it in his pocket. A king of shreds and patches. . . .

Gertrude screams.

Camera close on Hamlet as he sees the Ghost. During the following the voice of Gertrude and that of the Ghost are off camera, the latter being on echo chamber.

HAMLET:

What would your gracious figure?

GERTRUDE:

Alas, he's mad.

HAMLET:

O, say!

GHOST:

Do not forget. This visitation is but to whet thy almost blunted purpose.

Two-shot of Hamlet and Gertrude

HAMLET:

How is it with you, Lady?

GERTRUDE:

Alas, how is't with you.

HAMLET:

Do you see nothing there?

GERTRUDE:

Nothing at all; yet all that is I see.

HAMLET:

Nor did you nothing hear?

GERTRUDE:

No, nothing but ourselves.

HAMLET:

Why, look you there! Look how it steals away!

GERTRUDE:

This is the very coinage of your brain.

HAMLET:

It is not madness that I have uttered. Mother, confess yourself to heaven, repent what's past, avoid what is to come, and do not spread the compost on the weeds to make them ranker.

GERTRUDE:

O Hamlet, thou hast cleft my heart in twain.

HAMLET:

O, Mother, throw away the worser part of it, and live the purer with the other half. Good night—but go not to my uncle's bed. Assume a virtue, if you have it not. Refrain to-night, and that shall lend a kind of easiness to the next abstinence; the next more easy. Once more, good night, and when you are desirous to be blest, I'll blessing beg of you. So again, good night. I must be cruel only to be kind. Thus bad begins, and worse remains behind.

During the following narration Hamlet exits slowly and in a moment Claudius enters, to read anxiety on the face of Gertrude.

NARRATOR:

Now Claudius, knowing it was he you meant to kill, has you exiled immediately to England, so you are not in Denmark when Laertes returns to find his father slain and his sister Ophelia in the pitiable state in which we find her now.

Long shot of Gertrude, Claudius, Laertes, and Ophelia, who enters singing in a state of madness.

LAERTES:

O rose of May, dear maid, kind sister, sweet Ophelia! O heavens, is't possible a young maid's wits should be as mortal as an old man's life?

OPHELIA:

They bore him barefaced on the bier
And in his grave rained many a tear—
Fare you well, my dove! There's rosemary,
that's for remembrance. Pray you, love,
remember. And there is pansies—that's
for thoughts. There's fennel for you,
and columbines. There's rue for you, and
here's some for me. We may call it herb
of grace o' Sundays. O, you must wear your
rue with a difference. There's a daisy.
Camera close on Ophelia
I would give you some violets, but they
withered all when my father died. They say
'e made a good end.
*Dolly back to long shot of Ophelia, Laertes, Claudius,
and Gertrude*
(Singing)
For bonny sweet Robin is all my joy.
God 'a' mercy on his soul!
And on all Christian souls, I pray God.
God be with you.
Ophelia exits and camera comes close on Laertes.

LAERTES:

And so have I a noble father lost, a sister driven into
desp'rate terms, but my revenge will come.
*Dissolve to long shot of Laertes, Claudius, and Ger-
trude, who enters upstage and moves slowly down toward
Laertes.*

NARRATOR:

You, Hamlet, now far at sea, cannot know the fate of
fair Ophelia.
Camera close on Gertrude

GERTRUDE:

One woe doth tread upon another's heel, so fast they follow. Your sister's drowned, Laertes.

During the following narration the camera holds on Gertrude then shifts to Laertes for his reaction, then changes to a two-shot of Laertes and Claudius, who are plotting together and, finally, shifts to a Gravedigger with his shovel, holding a skull that he is regarding.

NARRATOR:

Ophelia drowned, and by her own mad choice, and you, Prince Hamlet, are safely stowed in England, or so your mother and your uncle think, but in a storm at sea you have escaped and now send word to Claudius, the King, that you are back in Denmark. At news of this, Claudius and Laertes plot against your life. Laertes will anoint his sword with deadly venom and the king will prepare a poisoned drink for you. All this you cannot know, as with Horatio you wander homeward through the graveyard.

Camera widens to three-shot as Hamlet and Horatio enter to join the Gravedigger.

HAMLET:

That skull had a tongue in it, and could sing once.

HORATIO:

Whose was it?

GRAVEDIGGER:

This same skull, sir, was, sir—Yorick's skull, the king's jester.

HAMLET:

Let me see. Alas, poor Yorick! I knew him, Horatio.

Two-shot of Hamlet and Horatio

But soft awhile. Here comes the king—the queen, the courtiers. Who is this they follow?

Camera close on Gertrude as she strews flowers.

GERTRUDE:

Sweets to the sweet! Farewell. I hoped thou shouldst have been my Hamlet's wife. I thought thy bride-bed to have decked, sweet maid, and not have strewed thy grave.

Camera close on Hamlet

HAMLET:

The fair Ophelia.

Camera close on Laertes

LAERTES:

Now pile your dust upon the quick and dead till of this flat a mountain you have made to o'ertop old Pelion or the skyish head of blue Olympus.

Dolly back to medium shot including Laertes, Hamlet, Claudius, Gertrude, and Horatio

HAMLET:

What is he whose grief bears such an emphasis? This is I, Hamlet the Dane!

LAERTES:

The devil take thy soul!

HAMLET:

I prithee take thy fingers from my throat.

GERTRUDE:

Hamlet, Hamlet!

ALL:

Gentlemen!

HORATIO:

Good my lord, be quiet.

HAMLET:

Why, I will fight with him upon this theme until my eyelids will no longer wag.

GERTRUDE:

O my son, what theme?

HAMLET:

I loved Ophelia. Forty thousand brothers could not with all their quantity of love make up my sum. What wilt thou do for her?

CLAUDIUS:

O, he is mad, Laertes.

GERTRUDE:

For love of God, forbear him.

HAMLET:

But it is no matter. Let Hercules himself do what he may, the cat will mew, and dog will have his day.
Hamlet exits as others stand looking after him. Dissolve to two-shot of Hamlet and Horatio.

HAMLET:

But I am very sorry, good Horatio, that to Laertes I forgot myself.

HORATIO:

Peace, who comes here?
Camera widens to three-shot

OSRIC:

Sir, you know, Laertes has returned to court. The king, sir, hath said, sir, that in a dozen passes between yourself and him he shall not exceed you three hits; he hath laid on twelve for nine, and it would come to immediate trial if your lordship would vouchsafe the answer.

HAMLET:

Let the foils be brought, the gentlemen willing, and the king hold his purpose, I will win for him as I can.
During the following narration the camera dissolves to a one-shot of Claudius, who is filling goblets from a decanter. He carefully puts one goblet to one side.

NARRATOR:

Is it desperation, despair, or procrastination—what is it,

Hamlet, that diverts you from your purpose? You know
you must avenge your father's death, you know your
uncle must be killed, yet you accept diversion.

CLAUDIUS:

Stay, give me drink. Hamlet, this pearl is thine.

*As Claudius drops pearl into the goblet, camera dollies
back for long shot including Claudius, Gertrude, Hamlet,
Horatio, and Laertes*

Here's to thy health. Give him the cup.

HAMLET:

I'll play this bout first; set it by awhile. Come, sir.

They engage in sword play.

Another hit. What say you?

LAERTES:

A touch, a touch; I do confess't.

GERTRUDE:

Here, Hamlet, take my napkin, rub thy brows.

The queen carouses to thy fortune, Hamlet.

HAMLET:

Good madam!

*The Queen drinks from the goblet that Claudius has
prepared for Hamlet.*

CLAUDIUS:

It is the poisoned cup; it is too late.

*Camera follows Hamlet and Laertes as they resume
their fencing. During the following narration Hamlet
is wounded but immediately disarms Laertes. Examin-
ing his wound, Hamlet puts down his sword and in the
confusion that follows Laertes mistakes Hamlet's sword
for his own. Now armed with Laertes' sword, Hamlet
wounds Laertes.*

NARRATOR:

You, Hamlet, are wounded, only a scratch, 'tis nothing,

or so you think. And in the confusion that follows, you
and Laertes unwittingly trade swords. So when you
now thrust home it is with the sword of Laertes.
*As Laertes falls, camera dollies back to long shot in-
cluding all the others.*

LAERTES:

I am justly killed with mine own treachery.

Gertrude falls into throne

CLAUDIUS:

She swoons to see them bleed.

GERTRUDE:

No, no, the drink, the drink! O my dear Hamlet!
The drink, the drink! I am poisoned.

HAMLET:

O villainy! Ho! let the door be locked.
Treachery! Seek it out.

LAERTES:

It is here, Hamlet.

Two-shot of Hamlet and Laertes

Hamlet, thou art slain; no med'cine in the world can
do thee good. In thee there is not half an hour's life.
The treacherous instrument is in thy hand, unbated and
envenomed. The foul practice hath turned itself on
me. Lo, here I lie, never to rise again. Thy mother's
poisoned. I can no more. The king, the king's to blame!

*Camera close on Hamlet as he thrusts the sword, pre-
sumably at the King who remains off camera.*

HAMLET:

Then, venom, do thy work!

*Two-shot of Hamlet and Claudius as Hamlet forces
the wounded King to drink from the poisoned cup.*

Here, thou incestuous, murd'rous, damned Dane, drink
off this potion. Is thy union here? Follow my mother.

LAERTES:

He is justly served. It is a poison tempered by himself.
Camera close on Laertes
Exchange forgiveness with me, noble Hamlet. Mine
and my father's death come not upon thee, nor thine
on me!
Camera close on Hamlet

HAMLET:

Heaven make thee free of it! I follow thee.
Two-shot of Hamlet and Horatio
I am dead, Horatio. If thou didst ever hold me in thy
heart, absent thee from felicity awhile, and in this
harsh world draw thy breath in pain, to tell my story.
O, I die, Horatio! The potent poison quite o'ercrows
my spirit. . . . The rest is silence.

HORATIO:

Now cracks a noble heart. Good night, sweet prince,
and flights of angels sing thee to thy rest!
Slow fade

Curtain

6
OTHELLO

OTHELLO

Othello

Synopsis

Why is it that man will sometimes kill the one he loves? Shakespeare grapples with that question in *Othello*. The answer in Othello's case is jealousy, but it is a jealousy implanted by that wickedest of villains, Iago.

Othello is a distinguished general, an esteemed and resplendent black man who has recently wooed and won the beautiful Desdemona, who has eloped with him. Iago and Cassio are Othello's high-ranking officers. Embittered by the rumor that Othello is about to promote Cassio instead of him, Iago is vengeful, and cunningly contrives to ruin the Moorish general, Othello, whom he professes to love with devout loyalty.

We are in Cypress long ago. Desdemona has just disembarked from her ship bearing her to Cypress and her eagerly waiting bridegroom. She is royally received by Cassio, Iago, and Emilia, Iago's wife and maid companion to Desdemona. Othello enters for a joyful reunion with his bride and they go quickly to his quarters, leaving Cassio and Iago to discuss the merits of the lady and toast her arrival.

Cassio, though reluctant to accept Iago's urging to drink freely to the occasion, drinks too freely and gets himself involved in a brawl, for which he is demoted by his esteemed Othello. Stinging from the disgrace of this, he is persuaded by Iago, pretending to befriend him, to solicit the help of Desdemona to bring him back into Othello's good graces.

Gracious Desdemona readily consents to plead his case, but the crafty Iago contrives to have Othello discover Cassio leaving the company of Desdemona, thus planting the seed of suspicion in Othello's mind. Suspicion grows when Desdemona tries to persuade Othello to reinstate Cassio and ask him to dine with them. Iago, later taking advantage of the situation, advises Othello to beware of jealousy, the green-eyed monster, all the while continuing to plant insidious seeds of suspicion.

Emilia innocently gives to her husband, Iago, as he has asked, a handkerchief that Desdemona has unknowingly dropped. He asks Othello if his bride has a handkerchief of such a description. Othello says that just such a handkerchief was his much-prized gift to his wife, with which she had promised never to part. Thereupon Iago says he has seen Cassio mopping his brow with that same handkerchief.

Alone with Desdemona, Othello asks for the handkerchief he gave her. When she cannot produce it, Othello's suspicion increases, while Desdemona unwittingly adds to his suspicion by continuing to plead Cassio's case.

Now Othello and Iago chance to see and hear a quarrel between Cassio and his paramour Bianca over a handkerchief that she has found in Cassio's room, the implication being that some other woman has been seeing Cassio, much to the annoyance of the paramour. Othello recognizes the handkerchief and is persuaded that she has betrayed him and has given it to Cassio.

This evidence, added to the crafty lies and insinua-

tions of Iago, convinces Othello that he must murder
his faithless wife. He orders Iago to bring poison to
him, but Iago suggests that to smother her in the bed
she has defiled would be much more appropriate. Othello
agrees and gives directions to Iago to do away with
Cassio.

Blinded with jealousy, Othello accuses his bride of
gross adultery and calls her "whore," a vilely insulting
word that Emilia overhears. When Othello has left
the room and Iago has entered, she declares this out-
rage to be the work of some sinister villain who has
poisoned the mind of the great, good general, whereupon
Iago swears there is no such man. Then, in a situation
of dramatic irony almost too much to bear, Desdemona
pleads with Iago to help her win back the confidence
and love of her husband. She does not see his smug
and sinister sneer or hear him say that this night will
either make or break him.

Exhausted with emotion and fearful of what may
happen next, Desdemona falls on her bed. Othello
comes to join her there and accuse her of adultery with
Cassio, saying that Cassio has confessed as much to Iago.
Desdemona begs that Cassio be summoned. She knows
he will deny that accusation because it is not true, but
Othello tells her Cassio is already dead. Then, at the
peak of his jealous rage, Othello smothers her, while
Emilia knocks at the door.

Emilia, herself, has dreadful news. "Cassio is dead,"
says Othello. No, it is a young Venetian who has been
killed by Cassio, who slew him in self-defense. Cassio
lives, but Desdemona is dead. Othello confesses it is he
who has killed her, killed her because she was false to
him. How could he ever have imagined such a thing?

What proof? What proof? In answer to Emilia's cries, Othello says it was her husband who gave him proof, his friend, her husband Iago, and there was the handkerchief as evidence. Emilia, almost beside herself, says is was she who gave the handkerchief to Iago, a handkerchief innocently dropped by Desdemona.

Iago has entered in time to realize that his treachery has been disclosed. Enraged, Othello lunges toward Iago with his sword, but Iago evades him, then kills Emilia. Cassio enters and knocks Iago's sword from his hand, then tells Othello that Iago has confessed to him that it was he, Iago, who had put the handkerchief in Cassio's room for his own evil purposes. Othello cries out, speaking of himself "O, fool, fool, fool. When you shall speak of me, then you must speak of one that lov'd not wisely, but too well." Then, in a burst of anguish, Othello stabs himself to death, and Cassio, aware of all the dead about him, turns to the cowering Iago with sword drawn and says, "Oh, Spartan dog! . . . this is thy work."

Othello

(Stage directions are in italics)

Note: A Narrator has not been created for this play. The characters themselves usurp his role.

CASSIO: *(Entering down right and addressing audience)*
Othello is the title of our play, and it was written by William Shakespeare nearly four centuries ago. I play the role of Michael Cassio, lieutenant to the great Venetian chief, Othello, the dark skinned, valiant Moor.
(Moves up right and looks off right)

IAGO: *(Entering down left and addressing audience)*
I like him not, this Michael Cassio. 'Tis said Othello plans to raise his rank to out-rank me.
(Moves down center)
I am Iago in the play. I hate the Moor, but will profess to love. Emilia, my wife and lady to Othello's bride, knows not my spiteful plot, nor shall she know.
(As he refers to her, Emilia enters down left)

EMILIA:
There are those men, who thinking evil thoughts, breed evil deeds. I wonder—sometimes I think Iago, my husband, such a man.

(During the above speech Iago focuses on Cassio)

CASSIO: *(Moving down right as Iago crosses to Emilia's right)*

In this abridgment of the bard's great play, we are at once in Cyprus, isle of charm. Fair Desdemona, bride of Othello, awaits arrival of her bridegroom lord. Her ship has docked and she has disembarked. *(Turning to greet Desdemona who enters up left and crosses up center)* Oh, behold, the riches of the ship have come on shore. *(Calling off right)* You men of Cyprus, let her have your knees. *(To Desdemona)* Hail to thee, Lady: and the grace of Heaven, Before, behind thee, and on every hand, Enwheel thee round. *(Kneels)*

DESDEMONA:

I thank you, valiant Cassio. What tidings can you tell me of my Lord?

CASSIO: *(Rising)*

Lo, where he comes.

OTHELLO: *(Entering up left and crossing to Desdemona's left)*

O, my fair warrior.

DESDEMONA:

My dear Othello.

OTHELLO:

It gives me wonder, great as my content,
To see you here before me. Oh, my soul's
joy, come! Let us to the Castle. Good
Michael, look you to the guard tonight.

CASSIO:

Iago hath direction what to do.

OTHELLO:

Iago is most honest.

Michael, good night. Come, my dear love.
Othello and Desdemona exeunt up right, Emilia follow-
ing.

CASSIO:
She's a most exquisite Lady.

IAGO:
And I'll warrant her, full of game.

CASSIO:
Indeed, she is a most fresh and delicate creature.

IAGO:
What an eye she has!
Methinks it sounds a parley to provocation.

CASSIO:
An inviting eye:
And yet methinks right modest.

IAGO:
And when she speaks,
Is it not an alarum to Love?

CASSIO:
She is indeed perfection.

IAGO:
Well: happiness to their sheets. Come, Lieutenant, I
have a stoup of wine, and here without are a brace of
Cyprus Gallants, that would fain have a measure to
the health of black Othello.

CASSIO:
Not tonight, good Iago, I have very poor and unhappy
brains for drinking.

IAGO:
But one cup. I'll drink for you.

CASSIO:
I have drunk but one cup tonight, and that was craftily

qualified too: and behold what innovation it makes here. I am unfortunate in the infirmity, and dare not task my weakness with any more.

IAGO:

What man? 'Tis a night of revels, the Gallants desire it.

CASSIO:

I'll do't, but it dislikes me.

Iago exits down left

CASSIO: *(Stepping out of character to address the audience)*

Here let us pause to say that Cassio, the character I play, imbibes too freely, and in a drunken brawl is provoked to anger, resulting in a fight and, for such conduct, he is relieved of his lieutenantship by his commanding officer, Othello.

IAGO: *(Reentering)*

What, are you hurt, Lieutenant?

CASSIO:

Ay, past all surgery!

IAGO:

Marry, God forbid.

CASSIO:

Reputation, reputation, reputation! I have lost my reputation. I have lost the immortal part of myself, and what remains is bestial. My reputation, Iago, my reputation! I will ask him for my place again, he shall tell me, I am a drunkard: Sir, I, drunk?

IAGO:

You, or any man living, may be drunk at a time, man. I tell you what you shall do: Our General's wife, is now the General. Confess yourself freely to her: Importune her help to put you in your place again. She is of so free, so kind, so apt, so blessed a disposition, she holds

it a vice in her goodness not to do more than she is
requested.

CASSIO:

You advise me well. Good night, honest Iago.

Exit Cassio up right

IAGO:

For whiles this honest fool
Plies Desdemona, to repair his fortune,
And she for him pleads strongly to the Moor,
I'll pour this pestilence into his ear:
That she repeals him, for her body's lust,
And by how much she strives to do him good,
She shall undo her credit with the Moor.
So will I turn her virtue into pitch,
And out of her own goodness make the net
That shall enmesh them all.

Iago exits down right
Desdemona, followed by Cassio and Emilia, enters up
right

DESDEMONA:

Be thou assur'd, good Cassio,
I will do all my abilities in thy behalf.

EMILIA:

Good Madam do: I warrant it grieves my husband
As if the cause were his.

DESDEMONA:

Oh that's an honest fellow: Do not doubt, Cassio,
But I will have my Lord and you again
As friendly as you were.

CASSIO:

Bounteous Madam,
Whatever shall become of Michael Cassio,
He's never anything but your true servant.

DESDEMONA:

I know't: I thank you: you do love my Lord:
You have known him long.
Before Emilia here, I give thee warrant of thy place.
Assure thee, if I do vow a friendship,
I'll perform it to the last article.
Therefore be merry, Cassio,
For thy solicitor shall rather die than give
thy cause away.

EMILIA:

Madam, here comes my Lord.

CASSIO:

Madam, I'll take my leave.

DESDEMONA:

Why stay, and hear me speak.

CASSIO:

Madam, not now: I am very ill at ease,
Unfit for mine own purposes.

Othello and Iago enter down right

DESDEMONA:

Well, do your discretion.

Exit Cassio down left

IAGO:

Hah? I like not that.

OTHELLO:

What dost thou say?

IAGO:

Nothing my Lord; or if—I know not what.

OTHELLO:

Was not that Cassio parted from my wife?

IAGO:

Cassio, my Lord? No sure, I cannot think it.
That he would steal away so guilty-like,

Seeing your coming.

OTHELLO:

I do believe 'twas he.

DESDEMONA:

How now, my Lord?
I have been talking with a suitor here,
A man that languishes in your displeasure.

OTHELLO:

Who is 't you mean?

DESDEMONA: *(Crossing to Othello)*

Why, your Lieutenant Cassio. Good my Lord, if I have
any grace or power to move you, his present reconcilia-
tion take. For if he be not one that truly loves you, that
errs in ignorance, and not in cunning, I have no judgment
in an honest face. I prithee call him back.

OTHELLO:

Went he hence now?

DESDEMONA:

Ay sooth; so humbled, that he hath left part of his
grief with me to suffer with him. Good Love, call him
back.

OTHELLO:

Now, now, sweet Desdemona, some other time.

DESDEMONA:

But shall 't be shortly?

OTHELLO:

The sooner, Sweet, for you.

DESDEMONA:

Shall't be tonight, at supper?

OTHELLO:

No, not tonight.

DESDEMONA:

Tomorrow dinner then?

OTHELLO:

I shall not dine at home: I meet the Captains at the Citadel.

DESDEMONA:

Why then tomorrow night, Tuesday morn, or Tuesday noon, or night; on Wednesday morn. I prithee name the time.

OTHELLO:

Prithee no more. Let him come when he will. I will deny thee nothing. Whereon, I do beseech thee, grant me this, to leave me but a little to myself.

DESDEMONA:

Shall I deny you? No: farewell, my Lord.

OTHELLO:

Farewell, my Desdemona.

Exeunt Desdemona and Emilia up left

Excellent wretch! Perdition catch my soul but I do love thee: and when I love thee not, Chaos is come again.

IAGO:

My noble Lord.

OTHELLO:

What dost thou say, Iago?

IAGO:

Did Michael Cassio, when you woo'd my Lady, know of your love?

OTHELLO:

He did, from first to last. Why dost thou ask?

IAGO:

But for a satisfaction of my thought,—no further harm.

OTHELLO:

Why of thy thought, Iago?

IAGO:

I did not think he had been acquainted with her.

OTHELLO:

O yes, and went between us very oft.

IAGO:

Indeed?

OTHELLO:

Indeed? Ay, indeed. Discern'st thou aught in that? Is he not honest?

IAGO:

Honest, my Lord?

OTHELLO:

Honest? Ay, honest.

IAGO:

My Lord, for aught I know.

OTHELLO:

What dost thou think?

IAGO:

Think, my Lord?

OTHELLO:

Think, my Lord? By Heaven, he echoes me; as if there were some monster in his thoughts too hideous to be shown. Thou didst mean something. I heard thee say even now, thou lik'st not that, when Cassio left my wife. What didst not like? And when I told thee, he was of my counsel, in my whole course of wooing, thou criest, Indeed?

IAGO:

For Michael Cassio I dare be sworn, I think that he is honest.

OTHELLO:

I think so, too.

IAGO:

Men should be what they seem,
Or those that be not, would they might seem none.

OTHELLO:

Certain, men should be what they seem.

IAGO:

Why then I think Cassio's an honest man.

OTHELLO:

Nay, yet there's more in this?
By Heaven I'll know thy thoughts.

IAGO:

Oh, beware, my Lord, of jealousy,
It is the green-ey'd monster, which doth mock the meat
it feeds on.

OTHELLO:

No, Iago, I'll see before I doubt; and when I doubt,
prove; and on the proof, there is no more but this, away
at once with love, or jealousy.

IAGO:

I am glad of this: For now I shall have reason to show
the love and duty that I bear you with franker spirit.
I speak not yet of proof. Look to your wife, observe
her well with Cassio, wear your eyes thus: not jealous,
nor secure. She did deceive her Father, marrying you.

OTHELLO:

And so she did.

IAGO:

I see this hath a little dash'd your spirits.

OTHELLO:

Not a jot, not a jot.

IAGO:

I' faith I fear it has. I hope you will consider what is
spoke comes from my love. But I do see y' are mov'd.
Cassio's my worthy friend. My Lord, I see y' are mov'd.

OTHELLO:

No, not much mov'd: I do not think but Desdemona's

honest.

IAGO:

Long live she so: and long live you to think so.

OTHELLO:

And yet how Nature erring from itself—

IAGO:

Ay, there's the point.

Iago exits down right

OTHELLO:

Farewell, farewell: If more thou dost perceive, let me know more: This honest creature doubtless sees and knows more than he unfolds. I had rather be a toad and live upon the vapour of a dungeon, than keep a corner in the thing I love for others' uses.

Othello exits down left

IAGO: *Entering down right as Emilia enters up left*

How now? What do you here alone?

EMILIA:

Do not you chide: I have a thing for you.

IAGO:

You have a thing for me? It is a common thing—

EMILIA:

Hah?

IAGO:

To have a foolish wife.

EMILIA:

Oh, is that all? What will you give me now for that same handkerchief?

IAGO:

What handkerchief?

EMILIA:

What handkerchief? Why that the Moor first gave

to Desdemona, that which so often you did bid me
steal.

IAGO:

Hast stolen it from her?

EMILIA:

No, faith, she let it drop by negligence, and to th'
advantage, I being here, took 't up: look here 'tis.

IAGO:

A good wench, give it me.

Iago takes handkerchief from her

EMILIA:

What will you do with 't, that you have been so earnest
to have me filch it?

IAGO:

Why, what is that to you?

EMILIA:

If it be not for some purpose of import, give 't me
again. Poor Lady, she'll run mad when she shall lack it.

IAGO:

Be not acknown on 't: I have use for it. Go, leave me.

Emilia exits up left as Othello enters down left

My Lord, have you not sometimes seen a handkerchief
spotted with strawberries, in your wife's hand?

OTHELLO:

I gave her such a one: 'twas my first gift.

IAGO:

I know not that. But such a handkerchief, I am sure it
was your wife's, did I today see Cassio wipe his beard
with.

OTHELLO:

If it be that—

IAGO:

If it be that, or any, it was hers. It speaks against her

with the other proofs.

OTHELLO:

Now do I see 'tis true. Come, go with me apart.

He moves down right with Iago, who exits down right

DESDEMONA: *(Entering up left with Emilia)*

Where should I lose the handkerchief, Emilia?

EMILIA:

I know not, Madam.

DESDEMONA:

Believe me, I had rather have lost my purse full of crusadoes. *(To Othello)* Come, now your promise.

OTHELLO:

What promise, Chuck?

DESDEMONA:

I have sent to bid Cassio come speak with you.

OTHELLO:

I have a salt and sorry rheum offends me: Lend me thy handkerchief.

DESDEMONA:

Here, my Lord.

OTHELLO:

That which I gave you.

DESDEMONA:

I have it not about me.

OTHELLO:

Not?

DESDEMONA:

No 'i faith, my Lord.

OTHELLO:

That's a fault. That handkerchief did an Egyptian to my Mother give. She was a charmer, and could almost read the thoughts of people. Is 't lost? Is 't gone? Speak!

Is it out o' th' way?

DESDEMONA:

Bless us!

OTHELLO:

Say you?

DESDEMONA:

It is not lost: but what if it were?

OTHELLO:

How?

DESDEMONA:

I say it is not lost.

OTHELLO:

Fetch 't; let me see 't.

DESDEMONA:

Why, so I can: but I will not now. This is a trick to put me from my suit. Pray you, let Cassio be receiv'd again.

OTHELLO:

Fetch me the handkerchief! My mind misgives.

DESDEMONA:

Come, come: You'll never meet a more sufficient man.

OTHELLO:

The handkerchief.

DESDEMONA:

A man that all his time hath founded his good fortunes on your love; shar'd dangers with you—

OTHELLO:

The handkerchief.

DESDEMONA:

In sooth, you are to blame.

OTHELLO:

Zounds!

Exit Othello up right

EMILIA:

Is not this man jealous?

DESDEMONA *(Crossing up left, followed by Emilia and exiting on speech)*

I ne'er saw this before. Sure, there's some wonder in this handkerchief.

OTHELLO: *(Entering up right with Iago)*

You speak of Cassio, you hint of Cassio, but hath he said anything?

IAGO:

He hath, my Lord, but be you well assur'd, no more than he'll unswear.

OTHELLO:

What hath he said?

IAGO:

Faith, that he did. I know not what he did.

OTHELLO:

What? What?

IAGO:

Lie.

OTHELLO:

With her?

IAGO:

With her? On her—what you will.

OTHELLO:

Dost thou mock me?

IAGO:

I mock you not, by Heaven: But look you, yonder he comes, and with his paramour. Hide we here and watch. *Iago and Othello hold up right*

CASSIO: *(Followed by Bianca, entering down left)*

What do you mean by this haunting of me?

BIANCA:

Let the devil and his dam haunt you: what did you mean by that same handkerchief, you gave me even now? I was a fine fool to take it: I must take out the work? A likely piece of work, that you should find it in your chamber, and know not who left it there. This is some minx's token, and I must take out the work? There, give it your hobbyhorse, wheresoever you had it; I'll take out no work on 't.

CASSIO:

How now, my sweet Bianca? How now? How now?

OTHELLO:

By Heaven, that should be my handkerchief.

BIANCA:

If you'll come to supper tonight you may. If you will not, come when you are next prepar'd for.

She exits down left followed by Cassio

IAGO:

And did you see the handkerchief?

OTHELLO:

Was that mine?

IAGO:

Yours by this hand. And to see how he prizes the foolish woman your wife—She gave it him, and he hath given it his whore.

OTHELLO:

My heart is turn'd to stone! I strike it, and it hurts my hand. Cuckold me?

IAGO:

Oh, 'tis foul in her.

OTHELLO:

With mine Officer?

IAGO:

That's fouler.

OTHELLO:

Get me some poison, Iago, this night. I'll not expostulate with her, lest her body and beauty unprovide my mind again. This night, Iago.

IAGO:

Do it not with poison. Strangle her in her bed, even the bed she hath contaminated.

OTHELLO:

Good, good! The justice of it pleases, very good. And within these three days let me hear thee say that Cassio's not alive.

IAGO:

As for Cassio, the night is dark, and young Roderigo hath a quick and ready sword. You will hear more by midnight.

OTHELLO:

Excellent. *(Calling) Desdemona!*
Iago exits down left

DESDEMONA: *(Entering up left)*

My Lord, what is your will? What is your pleasure?

OTHELLO:

Let me see your eyes: look in my face.

DESDEMONA:

What horrible fancy 's this? Upon my knee, what doth your speech import? I understand a fury in your words, but not the words.

OTHELLO:

Why? What art thou?

DESDEMONA:

Your wife, my Lord: your true and loyal wife.

OTHELLO:

Come, swear it, damn thyself.

DESDEMONA:

Heaven doth truly know it.

OTHELLO:

Heaven truly knows, that thou art false as hell!

DESDEMONA:

To whom, my Lord? With whom? How am I false?

OTHELLO:

Ah Desdemona, away, away, away!

DESDEMONA:

Alas, the heavy day! Why do you weep? Am I the motive of these tears, my Lord?

OTHELLO:

Would thou hadst ne'er been born.

DESDEMONA:

Alas, what ignorant sin have I committed?

OTHELLO:

Was this fair paper, this most goodly book made to write whore upon?

DESDEMONA:

By Heaven, you do me wrong!

OTHELLO:

Are you not a strumpet?

DESDEMONA:

No, as I am a Christian. If to preserve this vessel for my Lord from any hated foul unlawful touch be not to be a strumpet, I am none.

OTHELLO:

I cry you mercy then. I took you for that cunning whore of Venice that married with Othello. You Mistress, *(Enter Emilia up left)* that have the office opposite to Saint Peter, and keeps the gate of hell; you, you; ay you! We have done our course. There's money for your pains. I pray you turn the key, and keep our counsel! *Othello exits down right*

EMILIA:

Alas, what does this gentleman conceive? How do you, Madam? How do you, my good Lady?

DESDEMONA:

Faith, half asleep.

IAGO: *(Entering down left)*

What is the matter, Lady?

EMILIA:

Alas, Iago, my Lord hath so bewhor'd her, thrown such despite, and heavy terms upon her, that true heart cannot bear it.

DESDEMONA:

Am I that name, Iago?

IAGO:

What name, fair Lady?

DESDEMONA:

Such as she said my Lord did say I was.

EMILIA:

He called her whore! A beggar in his drink could not have laid such terms upon his callet.

IAGO:

Why did he so?

DESDEMONA:

I do not know; I am sure I am none such.

IAGO:

How comes this trick upon him?

DESDEMONA:

Nay, Heaven doth know.

EMILIA:

I will be hang'd, if some eternal villain, some busy and insinuating rogue, some cogging, cozening slave, to get some office, have not devis'd this slander! I will be hang'd else.

IAGO:

Fie, there is no such man; it is impossible.

DESDEMONA:

If any such there be, Heaven pardon him.

EMILIA:

A halter pardon him, and hell gnaw his bones. Why should he call her whore? Who keeps her company? What place? What time? What form? What likelihood?

DESDEMONA:

Alas Iago, what shall I do to win my Lord again? Good friend, go to him. For by this light of Heaven, I know not how I lost him. Here I kneel: if e'er my will did trespass 'gainst his love, either in discourse of thought or actual deed, or that mine eyes, mine ears, or any sense delighted them, or any other form. Or that I do not yet, and ever did, and ever will, though he do shake me off to beggarly divorcement, love him dearly— Comfort forswear me.

IAGO:

I pray you be content; 'tis but his humour. *(To himself)* This is the night that either makes me or fore-does me quite.

Iago exits down left

EMILIA:

Ay, would you had never seen him.

DESDEMONA:

So would not I. My love doth so approve him, that even his stubbornness, his checks, his frowns—
Knocking is heard
Hark, who is 't that knocks?

EMILIA:

It's the wind.

DESDEMONA:

O these men, these men! Dost thou in conscience think, tell me Emilia, that there be women do abuse their husbands in such gross kind?

EMILIA:

There be some such, no question.

DESDEMONA:

I do not think there is any such woman. Good night, good night. Heaven me such uses send, not to pick bad from bad, but by bad, mend.

Desdemona lies on sofa up center. Emilia exits down left.

OTHELLO: *(Entering down right)*

It is the cause, it is the cause, my soul. Put out the light, and then put out the light! She wakes.

DESDEMONA:

Who's there? Othello?

OTHELLO:

Ay, Desdemona.

DESDEMONA:

Will you come to bed, my Lord?

OTHELLO:

Have you pray'd tonight, Desdemona?

DESDEMONA:

Ay, my Lord.

OTHELLO:

I would not kill thy unprepared spirit. No, Heaven forfend, I would not kill thy soul.

DESDEMONA:

Talk you of killing?

OTHELLO:

Ay, I do.

DESDEMONA:

Then Heaven have mercy on me!

OTHELLO:

Amen, with all my heart.

DESDEMONA:

If you say so, I hope you will not kill me.

OTHELLO:

That handkerchief which I so lov'd, and gave thee, thou gav'st to Cassio.

DESDEMONA:

No, by my life and soul. Send for the man, and ask him.

OTHELLO:

Sweet soul, take heed, take heed of perjury; thou art on thy death-bed.

DESDEMONA:

O Heaven, have mercy on me!

OTHELLO:

I say, Amen.

DESDEMONA:

And you have mercy too. I never did offend you in my life; never lov'd Cassio, but with such general warranty of Heaven as I might love. I never gave him token.

OTHELLO:

By Heaven I saw my handkerchief in 's hand.

DESDEMONA:

He found it then; I never gave it him. Send for him hither, let him confess a truth.

OTHELLO:

He hath confess'd.

DESDEMONA:

What, my Lord?

OTHELLO:

That he hath us'd thee.

DESDEMONA:

How? Unlawfully?

OTHELLO:

Ay.

DESDEMONA:

He will not say so.

OTHELLO:

No: his mouth is stopp'd: honest Iago hath ta'en order for 't.

DESDEMONA:

Oh, my fear interprets. What, is he dead?

OTHELLO:

Had all his hairs been lives, my great revenge had stomach for them all.

DESDEMONA:

Alas, he is betray'd, and I undone!

OTHELLO:

Out, strumpet, weep'st thou for him to my face?

DESDEMONA:

O banish me my Lord, but kill me not.

OTHELLO:

Down, strumpet!

DESDEMONA:

Kill me tomorrow, let me live tonight.

OTHELLO:

Nay, if you strive.

DESDEMONA:

But half an hour.

OTHELLO:

Being done, there is no pause.

DESDEMONA:

But while I say one prayer.

OTHELLO:

It is too late. *(smothers her)*

Emilia calls from off left

EMILIA:

My Lord, my Lord? What hoa? My Lord, my Lord!

OTHELLO:

What noise is this? I think she stirs again. No,—what's best to do? If she come in, she'll sure speak to my wife. My wife, my wife—what wife? I have no wife.

EMILIA: *(still off stage)*

I do beseech you that I may speak with you. Good my Lord.

OTHELLO:

I had forgot thee: oh, come in, Emilia. Soft, by and by, let me the curtains draw. Where art thou? What's the matter with thee now?

EMILIA: *(entering down left)*

Oh, my good Lord, Cassio, my Lord, hath kill'd a young Venetian call'd Roderigo.

OTHELLO:

Roderigo kill'd? and Cassio kill'd?

EMILIA:

No, Cassio is not kill'd.

OTHELLO:

Not Cassio kill'd. Then murther 's out of tune.

DESDEMONA: *(weakly)*

O falsely, falsely murder'd.

EMILIA:

Out and alas, that was my Lady's voice! Help, help hoa, help!

Running to Desdemona and kneeling beside the sofa

Oh Lady, speak again, sweet Desdemona, oh sweet Mistress, speak.

DESDEMONA:

A guiltless death, I die.

EMILIA:

Oh, who hath done this deed?

DESDEMONA:

Nobody: I myself—farewell—Commend me to my kind Lord, oh—farewell. *(she dies)*

OTHELLO:

'Twas I that kill'd her.

EMILIA:

Oh, the more angel she, and you the blacker devil!

OTHELLO:

She was false as water.

EMILIA:

Thou art rash as fire, to say that she was false. Oh, she was heavenly true.

OTHELLO:

Cassio did top her. Ask thy husband else. Thy husband knew it all.

EMILIA:

My husband?

OTHELLO:

Thy husband.

EMILIA:

That she was false to wedlock?

OTHELLO:

Ay, with Cassio.

EMILIA:

My husband?

OTHELLO:

I say thy husband! Dost understand the word? My friend, thy husband; honest, honest Iago.

EMILIA:

He lies to th' heart! She was too fond of her most filthy bargain.

OTHELLO:

Hah? *(threatening Emilia)*

EMILIA:

Do thy worst! I'll make thee known, though I lost twenty lives! Help, help, hoa, help! The Moor hath kill'd my Mistress! Murther, murther!

IAGO:

(entering down left) What is the matter? How now, General. What is the matter?

EMILIA:

Disprove this villain, if thou be'st a man: He says thou told'st him that his wife was false: I know thou didst not, thou art not such a villain. Speak, for my heart is full.

IAGO:

I told him what I thought, and told no more than what he found himself was apt, and true.

EMILIA:

But did you ever tell him she was false?

IAGO:

I did.

EMILIA:

You told a lie, an odious damned lie! Upon my soul, a lie; a wicked lie! She false with Cassio? Did you say with Cassio?

IAGO:

With Cassio, Mistress! Go to, charm your tongue.

EMILIA:

I will not charm my tongue; I am bound to speak.

OTHELLO:

'Tis pitiful: but yet Iago knows that she with Cassio

hath the act of shame, a thousand times committed. Cassio confess'd it, and she did gratify his amorous works with that recognizance and pledge of love which I first gave her. I saw it in his hand. It was a handkerchief, an antique token my Father gave my Mother.

EMILIA:

Oh God! Oh thou dull Moor, that handkerchief thou speak'st of I found by fortune, and did give my husband.

OTHELLO:

Oh, fool, fool! Precious villain!

Othello rushes at Iago, who evades him. Iago then kills Emilia.

CASSIO: *(Entering up left to knock the sword from Iago's hand and hold him at bay)* Foul villain. Miserable wretch. Thou hast killed thy wife!

OTHELLO:

Are there no stones in Heaven, but what serves for the thunder? How came you, Cassio, by that handkerchief that was my wife's?

CASSIO:

I found it in my chamber. And Iago hath since confess'd to me that there he dropp'd it for a special purpose which wrought to his desire.

OTHELLO:

O fool, fool, fool! When you shall speak of me, then must you speak of one that lov'd not wisely, but too well. Of one whose hand, like the base Indian, threw a pearl away richer than all his tribe. Set you down this, and say besides, that in Aleppo once, where a malignant and a turban'd Turk beat a Venetian and traduc'd the State, I took by th' throat the circumcised dog and smote him, thus.

He stabs himself

CASSIO:

Oh, Spartan dog! More fell than anguish, hunger, or the sea! Look on the tragic loading of this bed: this is thy work.

Curtain

APPENDIX

A. Who Was Shakespeare?

B. Shakespeare's England

Who Was Shakespeare?

If, through some science fiction contraption, we could go back four centuries to the England of Elizabeth the First and ask to see an actor called Will Shakespeare, we might uncover many facts that posterity has not bothered to preserve. Actually, so few facts are known about the man William Shakespeare, that one wonders why that name is one of the most renowned and most revered names in the entire civilized world.

That such a man as Shakespeare did exist is evidenced by appallingly few historical facts. The facts are these: on, or near, the twenty-third of April, 1564, a son was born to Mary Shakespeare, wife of a glove maker, living in the bustling little town of Stratford on the river Avon not far from London. The father, John Shakespeare, was a town burgher and a prominent Stratford citizen. The son was christened William, and, although it is easy to assume that he grew up with the care and schooling common to the lads of English tradesmen of his time, we have no further record of young William until 1582 when, at the age of eighteen or thereabouts, he was married to Ann Hathaway, who was some eight years his senior and who subsequently bore him three children. They were Susanna, born May 26, 1583, and the twins Hamnet and Judith, born on February 2, 1585.

Later young Will turned up in London. The playwright Robert Greene, writing of the theatre activities of that period, refers to an actor named William Shakespeare who had recently taken to writing plays. Greene's reference was to a line from Shakespeare's King Henry VI, Part 3, suggesting that the "actor turned playwright" had been in London long enough to write parts 1 and 2 prior to the 1592 date.

It is likely that Shakespeare acted with and wrote for several acting companies of the Elizabethan period. Records show that in 1594 he joined the Lord Chamberlain's Company, and it is presumed that he remained with it until his retirement. Records show, too, that he was part owner of the then-famous Globe Theatre, and that his plays and sonnets were becoming popular.

Other legal records indicate that he applied successfully for a family coat of arms in 1596; that he purchased expensive property in Stratford in 1597 and in London in 1613; and that he made out his will on March 25, 1616, leaving his real estate to his eldest daughter, Susanna, and substantial sums of money to his only other surviving child, Judith. The date of his death is recorded as April 23, 1616, presumably his birthday.

The rest is legend, all but the plays and the poems. The sonnets are thought to have been written during the 1590's, but addressed to whom nobody knows for certain. Some think even the Queen. But those thirty-six plays and 154 sonnets that bear his name have rocked the literary and the theatrical world as nothing else has ever done since the creation of the Bible.

Did Ann and the children ever live with Will in London? No one knows. Facts do not warrant an assumption of an estrangement between Will and Ann. Will may have kept in close touch with his family and may have made frequent visits to Stratford. He must have been in Stratford some time in 1597 to purchase New Place, one of Stratford's principal dwellings. The purchase of such a commodious property suggests that he may have been looking forward to retirement in the quiet environment of his birthplace, but he hit his peak after the turn of the century. *Hamlet, Macbeth, Othello, King Lear,* and *Twelfth Night* all belong to that period. It was probably a period of affluence for Will. He retired in 1610 or 1611, possibly because of poor health, a yearning for a quiet life, a desire to be with his family, or an inability or an unwillingness to accommodate to the changing tastes of the theatre-going public.

How a small-town youth with no university training, no travel abroad, and limited experience could succeed so brilliantly in the sophisticated city of London, to say nothing of turning out play after play, each of which was a hit with the highly critical public and each a lasting literary gem pregnant with poetic image, philosophy, humor, history, and the gamut of human emotions, is one of the great wonders of the ages, a wonder that continues to baffle the wisest of men.

There were contemporaries of Shakespeare who wrote more plays. Lope de Vega, for example, a Spanish playwright who outlived Shakespeare by twenty years, wrote some three hundred pieces for the stage. But Shakespeare, by all accounts, was an actor, and presumably did most of his writing after performance hours and between engagements, writing in alehouses, legend has it, or backstage at the famous Globe Theatre.

It is easy to see why people, some of them reputable scholars, have asked and continue to ask "Who really wrote the plays of Shakespeare?" The controversial question has prompted much research and provoked the writing of many books and learned dissertations, some trying to prove that Francis Bacon was author of the

Shakespearean plays, others that Kit Marlowe was the author, still others trying to prove that the plays and sonnets were written by Sir Walter Raleigh, the Earls of Oxford, Derby, Rutland, and Essex. In all, some fifty-seven persons have been credited with the authorship of Shakespeare's plays.

One wonders how a prolific writer on jurisprudence, science, and philosophy such as Francis Bacon could have found time in his very active life to write so many plays any more than could have a busy actor, or how a man with Bacon's specialized training could have learned so much about the theatre, but nevertheless, Sir Francis Bacon continues to have his champions. Kit Marlowe, a very competent contemporary playwright remembered for his *Dr. Faustus,* was allegedly killed in a tavern brawl in 1593 while still a young man, but his contenders proceed on the assumption that he was spirited away instead of being killed, and continued to write in seclusion and under the name of William Shakespeare. But anyone who knows much about playwriting knows that the author needs to be on hand for rehearsals, because plays are not merely written. They are rewritten, with changes being made even after the opening performance.

Those who contend that no one man could have had the wide and diverse knowledge evidenced in the Shakespearean plays, insist that the plays were written by a group of writers, or at least a team, much as screen plays are often put together nowadays. Until more exacting historical evidence is discovered, none of these theories can be entirely proved or disproved. However, two facts seem to certify rather soundly Shakespeare's authorship. William Shakespeare is referred to extensively both as actor and playwright in letters and records of the Elizabethean period. There was obviously no question about the authorship of the plays when most of them were first published, only seven years after Shakespeare's death. Furthermore, incredible and versatile genius has been evidenced at other times by such persons as Aristotle, Michaelangelo, Leonardo da Vinci, Benjamin Franklin, and Albert Schweitzer, so it can be plausibly assumed that a man of Shakespeare's stature could have existed.

There is ample and even abundant information to credit Shakespeare as the great, incomparable dramatist and poet time and tradition have made of him, although it seems most likely that he may have had assistance in research and much advice from members of his company and from experts in special areas.

Judging from the tolerance and great-hearted understanding so evident in all of Shakespeare's plays, it seems safe to assume that he was a man who listened to good counsel, and judging from the keen sense of dramatic values also apparent in his plays, he was probably willing enough to make alterations in his scripts that would enrich his characters or heighten theatrical impact. This is not to suggest that the Bard from Stratford was a mere brain picker, or that his judgment was not always ultimately final, but it must be remembered that he was writing for the theatre, not the library or the classroom, and anything the audience did not like was either scrapped or revised.

Scholars who ponder over hidden meanings in the texts of the plays, teachers who approach the plays purely as literature, and students who become engrossed in similes, metaphors, obscure references, and footnotes, are likely to think of Shakespeare as a scholarly genius pedantically rendering his compositions in a lonely ivory-tower seclusion, instead of as a dynamic full-blooded writer for actors who was forever trying to meet a deadline.

Certainly a scholarly approach to Shakespeare is both commendable and needed, but it should be remembered that he wrote not for posterity but for the theatre patrons and the groundlings. Ever mindful of those people out front, Shakespeare has Hamlet admonish the Players not to split the ears of groundlings, and in the Prologue to Henry V, the first play he wrote after the opening of the new Globe Theatre, he takes the audience in by apologizing for the limits of the stage.

It is one of history's most lamentable ironies that posterity should know so little about the life of the man who gave life new dimension. Probably Gentle Will, as he was known to his friends, never thought of himself as having any significance to future generations and apparently never thought of his plays as having any value beyond their contemporary usefulness, since they remained in handwritten manuscript throughout his lifetime and were not included as properties in his last will and testament. The art of the theatre being an ephemeral thing at best, it seems likely that Shakespeare, like Richard Burbage, Will Kemp, and others of his company, was completely absorbed in succeeding with the show business of his time, which, even in its heyday, was a precarious enterprise. It may be, too, that Shakespeare lost whatever interest he might have had in posterity when his only son, Hamnet, died while still a youth. Though he and Ann had two other children, they were daughters, and the loss of Hamnet meant there would be no heir to the Shakespeare name.

Soon after a farewell meeting with his fellow playwright, Ben Jonson, Shakespeare died, April 23, 1616. According to an account recorded by John Ward, Vicar of Stratford from 1662-1681, "Shakespeare, Drayton, and Ben Jonson had a merry meeting, and, it seems, drank too hard, for Shakespeare died of a fever there contracted."

Shakespeare's remains were interred under the floor of the chancel of Holy Trinity Church, the parish church of Stratford, just inside the altar rail. Some time between 1616 and 1622 a monument was erected on the north wall of the chancel not far from the gravestone. It was the work of Garret Johnson, one of the best of his trade. It shows superior workmanship and is characteristic of Will. It was probably based on a life mask. This is the famous Stratford bust, considered a faithful representation.

Never dreaming that his words would be immortal, and perhaps never even wishing that they might be, Shakespeare may have summed up, succinctly, all he had to say about the matter in the last speech of the last play he ever wrote before he turned his back on London, and some time prior to his fiftieth year headed home to Stratford. His final words in his farewell play he gave to Prospero, worker of spells in that play of pure enchantment, *The Tempest*. Ending the magic of his own make-believe, he declared:

"But this rough magic I here abjure . . . And deeper than did ever plummet sound, I'll drown my book."

Shakespeare's England

It was a boisterous, bustling, progressive place, that England of Shakespeare's time. For a century and more the trade guilds had been meeting the material needs of Englishmen and finding time to present their Cycle plays each year, plays that were biblical in nature but rich with comedy, plays that gave gainful employment to actors and stage mechanics. There were amateur actors, too, and many a public school revived the ancient plays of Greece and Rome and presented new plays by new playwrights. Activity abounded, and ideas filled the air: scientific, artistic, philosophic, and religious ideas. Many ideas came from France, Italy, and other countries of the Continent. Many were home grown. Some came from faraway America, where Sir Frances Drake and Sir Walter Raleigh were among England's new explorers. Elizabeth the First, the celebrated Queen, encouraged exploration, not only of the new-found West but of the minds of men. Even the frequent clashing of ideas was not frowned upon. Men of science such as Sir Francis Bacon could write their thoughts. Artists could express themselves in song and spoken words. Even the Puritans, who spurned the Church of England, were treated with some tolerance. Although it was no paradise for individual man, man as an individual felt his identity and strove boldly for self-expression.

It was a vigorous time and a time of violence. Men lived by the sword and worked with wits and hands to stay alive. There was game to be had in the forests for the shooting of an arrow. There were crops to be coaxed from the fields. There were trades to follow and a few professions, shops to keep, inns and ale houses, and services for the Court and for the common people.

Already conscious of a heritage that dated back five hundred years to the Magna Carta and even further, Englishmen were proud of their emerging nation and were ambitious to vie with Spain to become a world empire. It was a time of empire building, and the patriotic spirit of nationalism was a virture of the time. Yet it was a time also of soul searching, and soul stretching, as Englishmen sought ways to worship God according to the dictates of their consciences. Souls stretched, also by means of artistic expression, as England felt the full impact of the revival of learning begun two centuries earlier in Italy. Much of that expression could be seen in the theatres of London, which, though banned from London proper by the stodgy governing council, throve on the outskirts with the full blessing of the Queen and later her successor, James the First. James Burbage, an actor with a talent for carpentry, built the first theatre in 1476 and called it, simply, The Theatre.

News of that venture may well have reached Stratford on the river Avon, where a thirteen-year-old lad named William Shakespeare was, no doubt, learning about drama from his Latin school books. Likely enough, too, the young genius may have had his imagination excitingly ignited when the Burbage Company of players appeared in Stratford on one of their barnstorming tours. In any event, there was something in the English air that drew talented young men to London where playwrights and actors were active in a half a dozen theatres by the turn of the century.

At that time attendance at the theatre was not a matter of ordering tickets in advance, struggling through traffic, and surmounting the frustrations of finding a place to park. Instead, one walked or went by horseback, if he were fortunate enough to own a horse, or if he were quite rich, he went in his private horse-drawn coach. At the door of the theatre he paid a penny to join the groundlings standing in the area now known as the orchestra section, or as much as a shilling to sit in the balcony. The groundlings, though always important to the actors because they made up the greater part of the audience, were facetiously referred to as "Penny Stinkers." Bathtubs and showers had not yet been invented. The balcony was for lords and ladies; sometimes dandies who were more interested in being seen than in seeing the play would pay extra to sit on the stage just out of range of the actors.

If the people of that period were wantonly unwashed, they were also cold and hungry. Most of the common people of England never got quite enough to eat, and, since they had no central heating, most people were rarely warm enough except in the summer months, when they were often much too warm. No air conditioning!

At the theatre one might gain some relief from cold and hunger by huddling together and eating the fruits and goodies sold by the ever-present Orange Girls. Those vigorous vending wenches were almost as much a part of the theatre as the actors, and certainly were better known than the playwrights, who were usually the last to receive credit for their creative efforts. There were no opening-night critics, no reviewers from the daily press, and no daily press, so the man who wrote the play was usually known only to the players and directors, and, more often than not, as in Shakespeare's case, he was actually one of them. In fact, it was by acting and staging the plays that the playwrights of the period learned to write. This was no doubt true even of those more scholarly gentlemen with university degrees, such as Ben Jonson and Christopher Marlowe, who were actually better known in their time than was Will Shakespeare.

With no newspapers and with few written works finding their way into permanent print, and since plays were written purely for immediate performance, it is a great wonder that as many of the Elizabethan plays survive as do. Always an ephemeral thing at best, the performance of a play was remembered by those who performed it and those who saw it, but little thought was given to preserving the texts beyond the acting company's immediate need of them. It is to the eternal credit of some of his fellow actors that Shakespeare's plays were published at all. Shakespeare himself seems to have had no concern about his plays beyond their current usefulness. That he was writing great works of art, or gems of literature, or models for dramatists to follow through the centuries probably never crossed his mind. Nor did it occur to the publishers of his plays that they were being published for posterity. They were printed chiefly for the contemporary market. Genius, however, has a way of burning through, and the genius of the Elizabethan age still lights the world. Light, in both the physical and figurative sense, was an esteemed element in the England of Shakespeare. Not only were people hungry for the spiritual and intellectual light that they found in the entertainment of the theatre, but they were hampered by the lack of light that made daytime performances a necessity. Once the sun went down, London and all England, as indeed the rest of the world, settled into darkness except for such illumination as could be gleaned from candles, lamps, and torches.

All the playhouses in the fields adjacent to London—the Fortune, the Curtain, the Red Bull, and The Theatre itself—could offer only daytime entertainment, with plays starting shortly after noon and ending in time for the patrons to walk or drive back to their homes in the city before dark. This was true also of the Rose, the Swan, the Hope, and the Globe, which were across the Thames. The Globe, lest we forget, was Shakespeare's chief theatre. Although he was affiliated with other theatres, he was part owner of the Globe and had a hand in its erection in 1599.

Actually, the Globe was the old Burbage Theatre which, because of a wrongheeded denial of their lease, the Burbages, along with Shakespeare and others, tore down on Christmas Day, 1598, and carried across the river, piece by piece, to reassemble as the Globe. Even in those times theatrical managers had to figure ways to outwit uncooperative landlords.

The Burbages, who were good at outwitting the city officials, eventually acquired the use of a property that was under the direct control of the Crown and thus off-limits for the Puritanical London officials. The Crown had passed on to King James by the time the Burbages were able to work out a deal, but by 1609 they were in business in their new Blackfriars playhouse, a small, intimate place, just right for the elite audiences who would come paying premium admission prices. Furthermore, the Blackfriars was under cover, the first of the Elizabethan theatres that was not constructed around an open courtyard.

Again the enterprising Burbage family had scored

another innovation, in fact two innovations. Performances could now be given in the coldest weather, which
had not been the case in the open buildings, and night-
time presentations were within the realm of possibility.

There had been night performances for many years,
but they were limited to the great halls of castles and
a few of the more spacious inns. There, taper chandeliers
and rows of candles along the apron of the stage created
sufficient illumination, so this idea was transferred to the
Blackfriars, where four walls and a sturdy roof warded
off the gusts of wind and kept the candles free from
drafts.

All through the reigns of the good Queen Bess and
her successor, James I, only male actors appeared on
the stage. Female roles were taken by boys who played
such roles as Juliet, Ophelia, Portia, Katherine, and even
Lady Macbeth with such dramatic conviction that many
of them became celebrated favorites of the English audiences. Here let us add that all-boy performances were
frequently given by the boys' choirs of London and in
some of the provinces. Such presentations were often
given by such famous groups as the St. Paul and West-
minster choirs.

In the theaters of Shakespeare's time, boy actors
would often remain with the theatre company long
after they reached manhood, continuing then in adult
male roles. One such boy actor named Edward Kenniston
was still around years later when women started playing
female roles in the Restoration comedies encouraged by
Charles the Second in the late seventeenth century. Some
of the Restoration actresses gave a party in his honor
and he was considered by some to be the "prettiest"
among them.

With the enthronement of James the First in 1603,

the nature of theatrical productions began to change. King James was fond of spectacle, so, for the first time in this era of simple staging, realistic scenery was introduced. The plays of Shakespeare, Ben Jonson, Kit Marlowe, and their contemporaries were performed on a bare platform stage with virtually no scenery and only such properties as chairs, tables, thrones, and benches. New ideas began streaming in from Italy, where the art of painting perspective scenery had been developing for at least a century. In addition to realistic backdrops, such mechanical gadgetry as cloud effects, floating islands, erupting mountains, and flying chariots became box office attractions of the changing theatre.

Could Shakespeare change with this changing theatre? There is some evidence that he tried. In what is generally considered his last play, *The Tempest,* for example, he introduced a Masque, a kind of ballet, in which goddesses appeared and nymphs danced on a stage that must have been rigged with mechanics and special effects. Still, the shift of emphasis from the sheer magic of words to plays that depended on realistic scenery and clumsy machinery may have been one of the reasons why he left the theatre while still a relatively young man. It is believed that he left London, returning to his native Stratford, some time around 1610, some six years before his death in 1616. The theatre of Shakespeare's heyday had changed, and Shakespeare's England was changing as well. Soon the Puritans would take over and the theatres, so much a sparkling part of the height of the Renaissance, would be blacked out and all entertainment banned for years to come.

Shakespeare, as history has proved, was unique, but so was the England of his time. So, too, were his fellow

Englishmen. Could there ever have been a Shakespeare without such an England and such Englishmen? Steeped in a tradition of kings and kings' bloody battles, of common people pursuing paths of freedom, of violent deeds and deeds of grace and civilized civility, steeped in such traditions, the great and the humble came to the theatre eager to see their history reenacted, their tales of old retold, their humors tickled, and their souls refreshed. They needed no superfluous scenery to whet their imaginations. They heard in words and saw in action whatever they needed to follow the plays. A lighted candle told them it was night. A drum roll suggested ensuing battle, and the poetry of the text transported them to wherever the poet-playwright wanted them to be.

Let us take note of that phrase "poet-playwright." The dramatists of Shakespeare's England were poets. The Englishmen of Shakespeare's England had ears for poetry and souls that soared on the strong and virile verse. Indeed, we may conclude that in that singular time when Western civilization was being reborn, England herself was a majestic, epic poem.